225 Limericks

T. Rex Writes Limericks

Michael R. Slavit, Ph.D.

Copywrite © by 2022 Michael R. Slavit
Registration # TXu 2-318-094
All rights reserved.

ISBN: 979-8-9860153-2-3

Seattle: Amazon Independent Publishing Platform

Table of Contents

What on Earth is a Limerick?   page vi

Limericks and U.S. History

George Washington Sets the Stage	page 1
The Louisiana Purchase	page 2
The Lewis and Clark Expedition	page 3
The Slater Mill	page 4
The Monroe Doctrine	page 5
John Quincy Adams	page 6
Andrew Jackson and the Trail of Tears	page 7
The Gold Rush	page 9
Utopia and Utopian Experiments	page 11
Abraham Lincoln – Fight to Preserve the Union	page 12
The Post-Civil War Era	page 13
The Advent of the County Grange	page 15
President Grant	page 17
The Seneca Fall Convention	page 19
Manifest Destiny	page 21
Richard Hoe Invents Roary Printing Press	page 22
Riding the Rails – the Era of the Hobo	page 23
Thomas Edison and the Electric Light Bulb	page 25
Chester Arthur's Change in Stance	page 27
The Tunguska Explosion	page 28

Electric Refrigeration at Home	page 30
World War II	page 32
The Dust Bowl	page 32
Post-World War II and the Truman Doctrine	page 34
Our First Knowledge of the Ocean Floor	page 35

Jurassic Park   page 39

Jurassic Park II - The Lost World   page 49

Harry Potter   page 59

The Universe, Earth and Life

The Universe Begins	page 76
Edwin Hubble and the Expanding Universe	page 78
Nuclear Fusion in the Sun's Core	page 80
The Fate of our Sun	page 81
Massive Stars Create Heavy Elements	page 82
Interstellar Gas and Dust Condense	page 84
The Early Solar System	page 85
The Formation of the Moon	page 86
The Early Bombardment	page 87
The Late, Heavy Bombardment	page 88
Origin of Earth's Oceans	page 90
The Origin of Life	page 90

The Great Oxygenation Event	page 94
Snowball Earth	page 94
The Principle of Superposition	page 97
The Cambrian Explosion	page 98
The Ordovician Period	page 100
The Silurian Period	page 101
The Devonian Period	page 103
The Carboniferous Period	page 104
The Permian Period	page 105
The Triassic Period	page 107
The Jurassic Period	page 108
The Cretaceous Period	page 110
The Paleogene	page 112
The Neogene	page 113
The Pleistocene	page 116
The Holocene	page 117
The Anthopocene	page 119

Attention Deficit Disorder	page 121
Classic Star Trek	page 130
Star Trek: The Next Generation	page 133
Star Trek: Deep Space Nine	page 136
Star Trek: Voyager	page 139
Friends, Family and Others	page 142
Fantasia and T Rex	page 149

What is a Scientific Theory?	page 150
Can't You Drive Better than That?	page 152
Poem about the Camel	page 153
About the Author	page 155
References	page 157

What on Earth is a Limerick?

A limerick is a whimsical verse, with five lines. The rhyme scheme is AABBA. Lines 1,2 and 5 always rhyme with one another, as do lines 4 and 5. Although the name may possibly come from the county and city of Limerick in Ireland, there is no clear indication of this. The limerick may have roots in late nineteenth century. Edward Lear (1812-1888) was an English humorist and writer of nonsense poetry who popularized the form. The contemporary limerick usually depends on a pun or witticism, and is very often suggestive or bawdy.

This book is a compilation of 225 limericks that I have written. I have organized them into eight sections:

- U.S. history (limericks 1 to 34)
- Jurassic Park (limericks 35 to 61)
- Jurassic Park II: The Lost World (limericks 62 to 86)
- Harry Potter (limericks 87 to 123)
- Origins of the Universe, Sun, Earth and Life (limericks 124 to 163)

- Attention Deficit Disorder (limericks 164 to 179)
- Classic Star Trek (limericks 180 to 187)
- Star Trek: The Next Generation (limericks 188 to 196)
- Star Trek: Deep Space Nine (limericks 197 to 202)
- Star Trek: Voyager (limericks 203 to 211)
- Communication with Family, Friends and others (limericks 212 to 221)
- Fantasia and T Rex (limerick 222)
- What is a Scientific Theory? (limerick 223)
- Can't You Drive Better that? (limericks 224 to 225)
- Poem about the Camel

Some of the limericks in this book – primarily those concerning American history and those about the Universe, the Earth and Life – are serious and informative. Some are casual communications and some are whimsical.

When I first wrote the limericks in the Jurassic Park and Harry Potter sections, they were stand-alone limericks with no explanation. Later, I went back and wrote some narratives. Thus, if you read or saw these adventures a while ago and your memory has faded, or even if you have only a passing knowledge of them, the limericks should be enjoyable for you.

In the *U.S. History* section, and in the *Universe, Earth and Life* section, there are substantial explanations of the topic prior to the presentation of the limericks. While reading this book, you can expect to learn some facts and concepts about U.S. History and about the Universe, the Earth and Life. I hope the combination of information and whimsy will make these pages enjoyable and worthwhile.

Limericks and U.S. History

George Washington Sets the Stage

George Washington served as our first president from 1789 to 1797. As the country's first President, many of the actions he took did set important precedents. Democratic self-rule had been absent from the world for about 2100 years, since the Greek city-state of Athens, and there were those who wanted Washington to be king. But Washington and many of the founding fathers valued liberty and were determined to set up a government without an autocrat at the top.

George Washington left the presidency voluntarily and after two terms. This was virtually unprecedented in world history, and helped set the stage for one of the most remarkable aspects of American democracy: the peaceful transition of government after elections. We may take this for granted and not realize the enormous importance of this legacy of our first President.

Some wanted to make him our king.
He declined, said "I'll do no such thing."
There's been too much oppression.
My term's just a session.
To the world a new order let's bring.

The Louisiana Purchase

In 1800 Napoleon wrested control from Spain of the territory west of the Mississippi River. U.S. diplomat Robert Livingston went to Paris to negotiate a purchase of New Orleans to protect American commerce through that seaport. France was having difficulty maintaining control in Haiti and was facing war with Great Britain. Napoleon therefore needed funds, and Livingston was surprised when the French offered to sell the entire Louisiana Territory to the United States. President Jefferson made the deal and added 828,000 square miles to the young republic.

Conflicts in Europe did bubble.
And Napoleon surely had trouble.
"To support my commands
I shall sell you some lands."
And the size of our nation did double.

The Lewis and Clark Expedition

Today, you could explore the Louisiana Territory in the comfort of your home by using Google Earth. Even before the advent of that technology, reconnaissance by air became possible in the early years of the twentieth century. But a century earlier, in 1804, there were no roads, cars, railroads, or any other technology to make exploration easy. The Lewis and Clark Expedition, commissioned by President Thomas Jefferson, took twenty-eight months from 1804 through 1806. The expedition had bold goals: to gain geographic, botanical, meteorological and ethnographic knowledge. Despite its success and significance, it was not until the mid-twentieth century that the expedition was completely researched and celebrated.

It is one thing to make acquisition.
To make growth of our lands a tradition.
But we had to explore
Mountains, rivers and more.
Thus, the Lewis and Clark Expedition.

The Slater Mill and the Beginning of the Textile Industry in America

The industrial revolution began in England with the establishment of textile mills. Samuel Slater was an apprentice in England. When he left England and came to the new world, he was not allowed to bring plans for the machines with him, so he had to memorize them. Moses Brown of Providence hired Slater to produce machines to spin cotton yarn, using water power. Slater Mill, completed in Pawtucket, Rhode Island in 1793, was designated a National Historic Landmark in 1966.

It would happen sooner or later.
To the cotton demand we would cater.
For the first working mill
The credit will still
Go to Rhode Islander Samuel Slater.

The Monroe Doctrine

There was an important development during the second term of President James Monroe. During their era of conquest, the Spanish had claimed most of South and Central America. Spain was losing its hold on the region and many countries were declaring their independence. In 1823 Spain asked France and other European countries for help in reconquering this part of the world. President Monroe responded by declaring the opposition of the United States to any European country interfering in this hemisphere. Though the policy was written by Secretary of State John Quincy Adams, it became known as The Monroe Doctrine and has been a basic part of American policy to this day.

Listen Europe: I think you should know.
Said the President James Monroe.
If you seek acquisition.
We'll give opposition.
Here's a place you may no longer go.

John Quincy Adams: Secretary of State, President and Congressman

John Quincy Adams served the country in a variety of major roles. President Madison sent John Quincy to Europe in 1814, where he helped to write the peace treaty that ended the War of 1812. The next President, James Monroe, appointed Adams secretary of state, and Adams helped frame the Monroe Doctrine.

John Quincy Adams became President in 1824, and he asked Congress for a national university, roads, canals and a naval academy. Although these measures were eventually enacted, it was not under his presidency. He valued education, high ethics and his dignity, but was seen as cold did not relate well with Congress.

Though hurt when defeated for re-election in 1928, he answered the call when the state of Massachusetts elected him to Congress. Some people thought it a disgrace to serve in Congress after having been President. Adams did not agree, and served seventeen years in Congress. He fought against slavery, for civil rights and free speech, and he helped found the Smithsonian Institution. He died in office in 1848.

Though denied a new term at the top.
J.Q. Adams would serve and not stop.
In the Congress he'd serve.
And he did so with verve.
And the cause of free speech he'd not drop.

Andrew Jackson and the Trail of Tears

President Andrew Jackson's legacy is tarnished by his role in the forced relocation of Native American tribes east of the Mississippi. Millions of acres of land had been guaranteed to the Cherokee Indians under federal law, but the state of Georgia decided to remove the Cherokees. The U.S. Supreme Court decided in favor of the Cherokees, ruling that Georgia had no authority over tribal lands. But Andrew Jackson took no action when Georgia expelled them, stating that Chief Justice Marshall made the ruling and could enforce it. This led to the infamous Trail of Tears, in which thousands died on the trek. This is one of several events inspiring some historians to regard Jackson as an unlikely symbol of democracy.

The Cherokees said that their tribe.
Had rights to the lands they'd describe.
The Supreme Court agreed.
Justice Marshall decreed:
To remove them: an act he'd proscribe.

But Georgia was heartless and rude.
And the vile Trail of Tears then ensued.
Jackson said, "You endorse it."
"You can darn well enforce it."
With such actions his term was imbued.

The Gold Rush

On January 24, 1848, James Marshall was working in the Sacramento Valley, building a water-powered sawmill for John Sutter, founder of the colony of New Switzerland. Marshall found flakes of gold in the American River, and later recalled, "It made my heart thump, for I was certain it was gold." Marshall and Sutter tried to keep the discovery secret. But word got out, sparking the Gold Rush, one of most celebrated events of American history.

Throughout 1849, people around the United States were drawn by the promise of wealth. They borrowed money or spent their life savings to make the journey to California. Known as "Forty-niners," they traveled across the mountains or sailed around Cape Horn in their efforts to reach California's promise of fortune.

Millions of dollars' worth of the precious metal was extracted from the area during the Gold Rush. By the end of 1849, the non-native population of the California territory had risen from less than 1,000 to

100,000, and the Gold Rush hastened California's admission to the Union as the 31st state.

Note: I had to employ the Italian word "lento," meaning "played slowly," to complete the following limerick.

A man working near Sacramento.
Found more than a little memento.
He looked at the lump,
Said, "It made my heart thump."
And the word got out quickly, not lento.

The Gold Rush was an era of hopes, dreams and some fast fortunes. But it was also a time of lawlessness and violence. Some miners made fortunes, but most made ten-to-fifteen dollars per day. There were often handsome profits for entrepreneurs there to service the miners, including saloon keepers and suppliers of equipment such as picks and shovels. To this day, the term "pick and shovel play" describes an investment strategy that invests in the materials or equipment needed to bring new technologies or services to market.

To great fortune a few found the way.
Many more made just dollars a day.
They would not live in hovels
If they sold picks and shovels
An investment term still used today.

Utopia and Utopian Experiments

In the early sixteenth century Sir Thomas More published a work entitled *Utopia*. The title comes from Greek words "ou topas," meaning "nowhere." More's work consists of a series of conversations between a traveler and a citizen of a society that had some ideal characteristics. Though More's title implies he probably felt an ideal society is impossible, and though his work had tongue-in-cheek elements, *Utopia* nonetheless had a profound influence on thought three centuries later. In the mid-nineteenth century, there was a widespread belief in the perfectibility of human society. In the United States between 1825 and 1860, there were about one hundred planned utopian communities.

An author named Sir Thomas More.
Wrote a novel that wasn't a bore.
The Utopian theme
Led to many a dream.
To experiments still part of lore.

Abraham Lincoln and the Fight to Preserve the Union

Abraham Lincoln took office in 1961. The following four years were among the most disruptive years in the life of the country, and surely the most dangerous for its survival.

Lincoln is considered to have been a great President because of what he did during the Civil War. He was not without flaws and was not universally admired, but he was a sincere and effective communicator who inspired belief and confidence. The United States was the only significant democracy in the world, and

Lincoln was determined to save the Union. There was a grand principle at stake: the ability of free men to govern themselves. Lincoln managed to convey this principle and its importance to the general public, and this probably enabled the country to endure a disruptive and bloody civil war. Although the goal of abolishing slavery became central as the War progressed, Lincoln fought the Civil War initially to preserve the Union.

From his purpose he never did swerve.
Though he sure needed plenty of nerve.
For the war had a cost
Of many men lost.
But the Union he sure did preserve.

The Post-Civil War Era

President Lincoln's dream was to restore the Union peacefully and without revenge, and he made an impassioned plea for this at his re-election inaugural address. He did not live to actualize his dream. Five days after General Robert E. Lee surrendered to Lincoln's general, Ulysses Grant, Lincoln was shot and killed as he and his wife attended a play. Had Lincoln lived, he may have actualized his dream of re-uniting the country peacefully and without bitterness and revenge.

Andrew Johnson became President after Lincoln's death. Although Johnson agreed with Lincoln's idea of reuniting the country without revenge, he lacked Lincoln's ability. And, many forces lined up against that plan. Radical Republicans wanted the South to suffer for its secession and did not admit newly elected southerners to Congress. The South was also to blame for the conflict, as they passed cruel laws severely limiting the rights of blacks. Congress divided the South into military districts and placed them under military command. The atmosphere of enmity and conflict resulted in one of the more shameful episodes in the nation's history: the birth of the Ku Klux Clan. The clan intimidated and killed blacks, as well as northerners who had come to the South, whether they had come south to profit or to teach. Johnson made speeches asking for moderation, but he lacked Lincoln's ability to communicate and persuade.

It was Abraham Lincoln's intention
To unite us without cruel contention.
But after Abe died
Although Johnson tried,
What ensued was unbridled dissension.

The Advent of the County Grange

In the late nineteenth century farmers were doing extremely poorly, both economically and in the eyes of others. Thomas Jefferson had called farmers "God's chosen people," but in the late nineteenth century the words "hayseed" and "hick" were used and did not indicate such admiration.

Many factors limited the success of farmers in the late nineteenth century. More acres were under cultivation, and harvesting yields were up by a factor of about six since the advent of the McCormack reaper. Overproduction lowered the prices of crops, and tariffs resulted in higher prices for equipment. Farmers had to borrow money for land, equipment, seeds and day-to-day necessities, and financial institutions were not providing favorable interest rates.

Most farmers were in perpetual debt, with little hope to recover. In addition, there was social isolation as more people left rural areas for industrial work in cities, and there was a loss of social status. It was a dismal time for the farmer.

A Department of Agriculture employee named Oliver Hudson Kelley started "the Granger Movement." Kelley was distressed by the lack of sound agricultural practices, and in 1867 started an organization with the goal of bringing farmers together for educational and social purposes. It was called the Patrons of Husbandry. By the mid-1870s, nearly every state had at least one Grange, and national membership reached close to 800,000. Granges provided the venue from which sprang the Populist Party, as farmers and other workers organized to fight for a fairer system.

They had lots of grain to exchange.
And their tumble from favor was strange.
Then they did unite
And put up a good fight.
It began with the birth of the grange.

President Grant

Americans have a tendency to over value their military heroes, and this was the case with Ulysses S. Grant. Grant was trained at West Point, but when his commanding officer insisted that he either quit drinking or resign, he resigned. He was seen as a wastrel who drank too much and failed at employment. But when the Civil War began, the North needed trained officers. He was appointed as colonel, then to general, and in 1864 was given command of all the Union forces.

Grant succeeded as a General, though he was willing to lose many men to achieve victories. Nonetheless his victories led to the end of the Civil War, and he became a national hero. Grant had no interest in politics, but in 1868 the Republican Party made him their nominee for President. As military leaders often capture the public's imagination, he was easily elected. Grant's presidency is usually considered by historians to have been a disaster. It was not due to a lack of desire on his part to be a good president, but rather due to lack of ability and, especially, to poor judgment in appointing officials. His administration was riddled with corruption, but Grant would not believe that the corruption was going on, even when he was apprised of it.

Grant did strive to reduce racial injustice, and some historians have referred to him as "the first civil rights president." And he did manage a few accomplishments of note through his Secretary of State Hamilton Fish. Secretary Fish helped avoid an untimely war with Spain and resolved some major issues with Great Britain.

He had served in the war with success.
But his presidency was a mess.
For he was surrounded
By officials not grounded
In good will or ethics, I guess.

The Seneca Falls Convention and the Equal Voting Rights Movement

Lucretia Mott and Elizabeth Cady Stanton met at the 1840 World Anti-Slavery Convention in London. As women, Mott and Stanton were barred from the London convention floor. This indignity motivated them to found the women's rights movement in the United States, and they organized the first women's rights convention held in the States. In July 1848 two hundred women convened in Seneca Falls. Elizabeth Stanton read a document she had drafted entitled "Declaration of Sentiments and Grievances," which followed the ideas of the U.S. Declaration of Independence. Its preamble stated, "We hold these truths to be self-evident: that all men and women are created equal . . . " The Declaration called upon women to organize and to petition for their rights.

The convention adopted the Declaration of Sentiments and Grievances and passed 12 resolutions calling for equal rights for women. All twelve resolutions passed, though the resolution calling for women's right to vote sparked lengthy debate. Some people ridiculed the idea of women's right to vote, but the resolution marked the beginning of the women's suffrage movement in America. Annual national woman's rights conventions were held, helping to fuel the women's suffrage movement. Finally, in 1920, seventy-two years after Seneca Falls, the nineteenth Amendment was adopted as part of the Progressive movement, and women had the constitutional right to vote.

E. C. Stanton and Lucretia Mott
Were not happy with most women's lot.
They raised some eyeballs
When at Seneca falls.
Their participants hatched a good plot.

They could have been passively scarred.
Having been from the London floor barred.
But they planned a convention.
To give women ascension.
And at the convention they starred.

Manifest Destiny

Manifest destiny was a term used to justify the mid-nineteenth century expansion of the United States' territory. The originator of this term is believed to have been news editor John O'Sullivan, and the phrase became popular. Though the term does not explicitly state it, the term "manifest destiny" implies that the expansion of the United States from the Atlantic to the Pacific was pre-ordained by fate or divine intention. The term lends a sense of lofty idealism to the push for expansion. *Manifest Destiny* justified the methods used to continue expansion, whether it was by war with Mexico or displacement of Indian tribes.

The United States would not rest
Till we'd reached the end of our quest.
It had burned like a fire
More land to acquire
'Twas our destiny, manifest.

Mexico's strength then was tested.
Many lands from its clutches were wrested.
Was it fair to provoke
Such a war, as did Polk?
Was it our destiny manifested?

Richard Hoe Invents the Rotary Printing Press

Newspapers were in operation in the early 1800s, but their printing methods were slow until Richard Hoe, an American inventor from New York City, designed a rotary printing press in 1843. Hoe's invention used a continuous roll of paper, enabled the printing of 8,000 newspapers per hour, and revolutionized newspaper publishing.

Hoe continued to innovate, and in 1870 developed a rotary press that printed both sides of a page in a single operation. Hoe's press fed eight hundred feet of paper per minute from a roll of paper five miles long. His apparatus included devices to cut and fold the pages for delivery. This process produced 18,000 papers an hour and was first used by the New York Tribune.

Printing papers was really quite slow
till the genius of one Richard Hoe.
We all must confess
That his rotary press
Did put many more folks "in the know."

Riding the Rails - the Era of the Hobo

After the Civil War, some discharged veterans hopped freight trains to return home. Others went west aboard trains seeking work on the frontier. Thousands of willing workers had no place in the post-Civil War economy. The migrant workers were at times called "bums" but more often called "hobos."

The era of the hobo spans the late nineteenth and early twentieth centuries. The era is commemorated in older songs such as The Wabash Cannonball and The Big Rock Candy Mountain. It is an era that has found its way into American folklore and film. There is an idealized view of the hobo, refusing to be tied down to routine, and seeking freedom and adventure on the rails. This is evidenced by Roger Miller's 1964 hit song: *King of the Road.* Miller's lyrics describe the life of a vagabond who is poor but revels in his freedom, whimsically calling himself "king of the road."

In reality, life as a hobo was difficult and dangerous. With no prospects at home, many traveled for free by freight train to try their luck. The itinerant worker was poor and far from home and support. Traveling in railroad boxcars was not safe. They could be trapped between cars, fall under the wheels trying to board, or could die of exposure in bad weather. In addition, railroad security staff had a reputation for violence against trespassers.

Historians estimate that hobos in the United States numbered about 500,000 in 1906 and increased to over a million during the Great Depression of the 1930s. The practice is less common today, though it still exists in folklore and song.

They rode on the rails for free.
It's not likely they did so with glee.
Though remembered in song
As intrepid and strong.
They were seen our country's debris.

Though their style may be seen as romantic.
It was so much more likely quite frantic.
They were riding the rail.
With their labor for sale.
And the perils they faced were gigantic.

Thomas Edison and the Electric Lightbulb

The importance of electric lighting cannot be overstated. Prior to artificial lighting, factories operated only by daylight. Thomas Edison was a prolific inventor who had over a thousand patents by the end of his career. In 1878, Edison focused on replacing the gaslight with a safe, inexpensive electric light – a goal scientists had pursued for 50 years
.

Edison set up the Edison Electric Light Company and began research. The invention of the lightbulb was difficult. Edison's idea was to pass electricity through a filament to make it glow, and to house the filament in a bulb with partial vacuum to slow the burning of the filament. He claimed to have tested thousands of vegetable growths, and to have "ransacked the world for the most suitable filament material." In 1880, he hit on carbonized bamboo as a viable material for the filament, which proved to be the key to a long-lasting and affordable light bulb. In 1881, he set up an electric light company. In 1904, European inventors found tungsten to be a better filament for incandescent lighting, and it became the standard. Electric lighting was a major factor as as the United States transitioned its primary economy and lifestyle from rural and agrarian to urban and industrial.

With darkness we had trouble fighting.
Was a candle sufficient for writing?
Thomas Edison
Provided the medicine.
The advent of electric lighting.

Chester Arthur's Change in Stance

Chester Arthur served as our 21st president from 1881 to 1885. Arthur's career and presidency may be seen as an example of how a person's values and beliefs can change. Politics in the mid-to-late 1800's were openly partisan and corrupt. Important jobs were handed out to men who supported the party in power, to which they in turn contributed money. This "spoils system" was accepted as common practice, and Arthur supported it. When James Garfield was nominated for the presidency, Arthur was a compromise nominee for Vice President. President Garfield wanted written examinations for government jobs as part of a reformed system in which people would be hired based on their qualifications. Chester Arthur, the stalwart, opposed Garfield. But President Garfield was murdered by a man who, after shooting him, shouted," I am a stalwart. Arthur is now President."

Arthur could not forget the reason for his predecessor's murder. As President, he felt a duty not just to his own party, but to all citizens. He attempted to carry on Garfield's proposed reforms, and asked Congress for a new civil service law. Stalwart politicians were angry at Arthur's change in stance, but a new civil service law was passed. Party stalwarts did not forgive Arthur and he was denied a nomination for a second term. He left office with the admiration of much of the nation. He is an example of an elected official rising to the challenge of his office and altering his stance to meet the needs of the people.

Politicians were very self-serving.
And the spoils system was quite unnerving.
For the system to mend.
Arthur sure bucked the trend.
Tried to give jobs to persons deserving.

The Tunguska Explosion

On June 30, 1908 there was a huge explosion near the Tunguska River in Siberia in the northern USSR. The blast levelled trees in an area of approximately 1500 square miles. Later expeditions to this remote area failed to locate a crater, which was a mystery, as the explosion was believed to have been caused by an impact. The incident started a series of celebrated rumors and legends, as some people speculated that the blast had been caused by an alien spaceship and others opined it had been caused by a tiny piece of antimatter. It is now known that large meteors or small asteroids will often, when they pass through Earth's atmosphere, explode above the Earth's surface. It is estimated that the meteor that caused the Tunguska event measured between 60 and 200 meters in diameter, and the explosion is estimated to have had the power of between 10 and 15 megatons and was at that time the largest explosion caused by a comet or meteor in recorded human history. We now know that there are thousands of so-called "near-Earth objects" in orbit about the Sun. The largest of them have been detected and their orbits have been calculated. The search continues.

In Tunguska in 1908.
An explosion whose power was great.
Levelled many a tree.
For explorers to see.
To-ten-megatons it did equate.

The shock wave would make you quite blistery.
Many tried to decipher its history.
No investigator
Found signs of a crater.
For years it remained a great mystery.

The blast left the landscape quite dreary.
And it kindled so many a theory!
Could it be a ship alien?
Were the pilots mammalian?
Speculation could make you quite weary.

On wild tales we place no reliance.
Telescopes are a better appliance.
A small asteroid.
Came to us from the void.
(Speculation did give way to science).

Electric Refrigeration at Home

There are so many conveniences in our lives that we take for granted. If we date the beginning of our nation to 1776, then we have been an independent nation for 246 years. For only ninety-five years – thirty-nine percent of our history – have we had refrigerators in our homes. During the nineteenth century, consumers preserved their food in iceboxes with ice purchased from ice harvesters. Consumers who used the icebox in 1910 had the same moldy, smelly situation that consumers had one hundred years earlier.

General Electric (GE) was one of the first companies to overcome these challenges. In 1927, GE released the first refrigerator that ran on electricity. In 1930 Frigidaire, a GE competitor, synthesized Freon, enabling the development of lighter, smaller, cheaper refrigerators. The average price of a refrigerator dropped from $275 to $154 with the synthesis of Freon. With this lower price, fifty percent of American households could afford refrigeration. Home life had thus taken a step toward resembling today's lifestyle.

For a century we'd been a nation
Without any refrigeration.
But GE used science.
Designed an appliance
And gave us a cooler sensation.

World War II

I am certainly not implying that so lengthy and complex a series of events as World War II can be summarized in a limerick. And, some historians warn us against over emphasizing the role of the United States in turning the tide of that war. Nonetheless Dwight Eisenhower did command Allied forces during the Normandy invasion. Thus, the following:

In Europe they wielded great power.
Though their fortunes would certainly sour.
To the Germans' surprise
There were stronger Allies
Led by General Dwight Eisenhower.

The Dust Bowl

A devastating series of dust storms took place in the U.S. and Canadian prairies in the 1930s and into 1940. The dust storms took place in three waves – 1934, 1936 and 1939-40 – and they were eventually termed "The Dust Bowl." A recent documentary describing history's ten worst weather-related disasters ranked the Dust Bowl as the most devastating of all.

The cause of the devastating dust storms was a lack of advanced agricultural methods. For years, farmers had used deep plowing of the virgin topsoil, displacing the deep-rooted grasses that had normally protected soil and moisture during periods of reduced rainfall. The unprotected soil turned into dust that was at the mercy of winds. It has been reported that huge clouds of dust blackened the sky. These events were termed "black blizzards" or "black rollers" that sometimes travelled as far as New York City and Washington. They not only devastated agriculture, but were an enormous health hazard. People could often not leave their homes without trying to cover their heads and faces, often to little avail. Dust choked cattle, and lung diseases were prevalent. Many families abandoned their farms and migrated. It is estimated that sixty percent of the population fled from the affected area.

The rich prairie soil was disarming.
The resulting event was alarming
Agriculture was dead.
Many families fled.
Due to ill-advised methods of farming.

Post-World War II and the Truman Doctrine

After World War II concluded, President Harry Truman, along with his Secretary of State George Marshall, developed the European Recovery Act, which came to be known as The Marshall Plan. It was announced on June 5, 1947. The goals of the plan were to rebuild war-torn areas, remove barriers to trade, modernize industry, and improve European prosperity. The United Kingdom, France and West Germany were the major recipients of United States aid.

Russia objected to what they saw as American interference in Europe and would not participate. During World War II, Russia and the United States had essentially been allies in defeating Hitler's Germany. But these two nations, the two most powerful in the post WWII era, would be on what historians saw as an inevitable collision course. Each saw expansion of the other as a threat.

On March 12, 1947 President Truman unveiled the Truman Doctrine, which stated that America's policy would be to stop Soviet expansion. Stopping the spread of non-democratic governments became the overriding aim of U.S. foreign policy until 2016.

By the late 40's we were assumin'
That a threat from the Russians was loomin'.
We embarked on a trek
To keep them in check
Per the doctrine of President Truman.

Our First Knowledge of the Ocean Floor

For years Earth scientists favored the concept of uniformitarianism, which stated that Earth has remained the same or has changed with extreme slowness. They believed the continents and oceans were as they had always been. However, if they had always been the same, then sand and silt washed into the oceans would have settled onto the ocean floors for eons. The ocean floors would thus be flat and featureless. Although Alfred Wegener had argued in 1912 that the continents move, he was ridiculed. Discoveries during and after World War II would vindicate Wegener and totally change our understanding of the Earth.

Harry Hess, geologist and Navy commander, had a mission to study the ocean floor for World War II military purposes. Ocean mapping via sonar revealed that the deep-sea floor was not a flat and featureless plain, but rather a dynamic landscape with vast mountain ranges, deep basins, and long trenches.

It had long been assumed that the floor
of the oceans was really a bore.
That view was repealed
When sonar revealed
There are mountains and trenches and more!

It is now known that Earth's crust is fractured and divided into plates that move. This is known as plate tectonics, the grand unifying theory of Earth science. The geological history of the Earth is essentially a history of the Earth slowly getting rid of the heat from its formation 4.6 billion years ago, as well as heat emitted by radioactive elements. Hot, molten rock rises from beneath the Earth's crust in the mid oceans to form new crust. This new crust is then forced away from the mid-ocean zone by even newer material rising from below. Hess and Robert S. Dietz, a scientist with the U.S. Coast and Geodetic Survey, coined the expression "seafloor spreading" to describe this process.

According to plate tectonics, the spreading oceanic crust is forced downward, or subducted, into the Earth along the leading edges of lighter continental crust. The descending oceanic crust melts at about 400 miles deep and becomes reabsorbed. The ocean basins are thus continually being recycled with the creation of new oceanic crust and the destruction of old crust. Keep in mind that the Earth's crust moves along at an average speed of about one inch per year. These changes thus require tens of millions of years. The discovery of the true nature of the ocean floor, of the Earth's crust and of plate tectonics has completely altered our understanding of our planet.

With a crust and a mantle and core.
Mother Earth is sure not a bore!
On the mantle, crust floats.
Not like ice cubes or boats.
In a year it moves one inch or more.

Jurassic Park

The premise of the story is that John Hammond, CEO of the Ingen Corporation, is building a spectacular wildlife park on a Costa Rican Island called Isla Nublar. The animals to be exhibited are dinosaurs. He has a team of scientists who have resurrected dinosaurs by using "dino DNA" extracted from amber. The idea is that mosquitoes would have fed on the blood of dinosaurs and would have landed on trees and become stuck in the sap, which later hardened as amber. Hammond's team of scientists collected amber, extracted the DNA, used super computers to analyze the DNA, filled in gene sequence gaps with frog DNA and, using ostrich eggs, hatched dinosaurs.

When we were both little and small.
Dino pictures were taped to our wall.
Our parents we'd vex.
With our talk of T-Rex.
Our fantasy life they'd enthrall.

For millions of years they did roam.
The whole of the Earth was their home.
When an asteroid struck
They were all out of luck
As the fossilized records have shown.

We've seen movies about them for years.
As children we'd greet them with cheers.
Their movements were choppy.
The artwork was sloppy.
The scientists must have shed tears!

CG is "compute" generation.
Providing enhanced animation.
The Park was Jurassic.
The movie's a classic.
It certainly caused a sensation.

To make us believe it could happen.
They couldn't be singin' or rappin'.
To induce our alliance.
They needed some science.
Into DNA lore they were tappin'.

They said that mosquitoes were biting.
On the dinosaurs they were alighting.
Along with some crud.
They would draw out some blood.
And that makes the story exciting.

The blueprints for animals livin'.
To the cells of the body are given.
The blueprint it dwells.
In the heart of all cells.
To discover those plans they were driven.

They displayed a scene they'd enacted.
In tree sap mosquitoes impacted.
In amber long buried.
Genetics were ferried.
Through years until it was extracted.

A worker was killed during an accident in the park. An insurance issue ensued. A lawyer representing Hammond's investors wanted an investigation of the stability of the park. To support his cause, Hammond hired three scientists: paleontologist Alan Grant, Grant's partner, paleobotanist Ellie Sattler, and mathematician (self-styled "chaotician") Ian Malcolm. The three scientists, along with attorney Donald Genaro and Hammond's two grandchildren, Lex and Tim, would be setting off in two remote-controlled vehicles, to tour the park.

They used DNA to build creatures.
For a park with superlative features.
Investors were wary.
To make it less scary.
They enlisted the help of some teachers.

To advance a convincing retort.
Hammond needed an expert report.
Doctors Sattler and Grant.
With their resources scant.
Agreed to give Hammond support.

One colleague, a mathematician.
Was intrusive and showed no contrition.
"It was chaos," he'd say.
That would surely hold sway.
And he criticized Hammond's ambition.

Dr. Sattler said "plants that you've picked,
Should not be touched, handled or licked"
"They're defensive" she said.
"They could make you quite dead."
If your skin were abraded or pricked.

At the table they each took a turn.
They explained what they hoped they would learn.
When the park they were touring.
They found it alluring.
Its dangers they'd quickly discern.

Hammond's Park was highly automated. His computer expert, Dennis Nedry, had underbid for the work and was upset at Hammond for not re-negotiating. Nedry was thus open to a bribe by a rival company who wanted Nedry to steal embryos for them. In order to steal and deliver the embryos, Nedry had to disable some park systems, including security. But he also disabled the tour vehicles as well as the electrified fences that contained the dinosaurs, and this led to T Rex breaking through the fence and wreaking havoc. When the T Rex approached the fence near the vehicle, Genaro fled from the van, leaving the door ajar, and ran into a nearby comfort station. It was growing dark and Lex found a flashlight and used it to see what was happening, and the light attracted Rex. When Tim closed the vehicle door, Rex looked closer, saw movement, and then attacked the van.

Hammond's grandchildren came for some fun.
They believed that the danger was none.
But short-lived was their bliss
As events went amiss.
When the tour had just barely begun.

A computer employee felt slighted.
To betray them he had been invited.
Hammond's rivals agreed.
To pay him for the deed.
And by bribes his sellout was incited.

To deliver the goods as arranged.
The security systems he changed.
When the game warden found.
Raptor prints on the ground
He concluded the guy was deranged.

With the doctors on tour in the van.
The catastrophe really began.
The computer guy, Dennis.
Created a menace.
To enact his nefarious plan.

His judgment was surely obtuse.
When his plans were to turn off the juice.
Non-electrified fence
Did not give a defense.
And T Rex was soon on the loose.

When the T Rex came close to the fence.
Genaro displayed no good sense.
He did flee from the van.
Went and sat on the can.
In a building for ladies and gents.

Lex and Tim were alone in the car.
But the front door had been left ajar.
Had they not flashed a light.
Things may have been right.
Rex would not see them from afar.

But by light T Rex was attracted.
An attack on the car she enacted.
But when Ian lit a flare.
And drew Rex out of there.
The kids then by Grant were extracted.

Ian was bold but not cunning.
With the flare from T Rex he was running.
Though some time he had bought
From behind he was caught.
And the impact was really quite stunning.

The outhouse was crumbled and beaten.
And I think this idea bears repeatin'.
Had Genaro lain flat.
Like a rug or a mat.
Then perhaps he would not have been eaten.

The only way to undo what Nedry had done was to shut down and re-start the park's computer system. Engineer Ray Arnold was reluctant, but Hammond convinced him it was their only hope. The shutdown did work, but kicked the circuit breakers. Game

Warden Robert Muldoon led Ellie to the maintenance shed, but lost his life in the process. Ellie did turn on the park's systems.

Dr. Grant led the children through the park and back to the visitors' center. Some velociraptors pursued them to the building, and Alan, Ellie, Lex and Tim had some harrowing moments before barely making their escape. They were saved by the Rex, who had also made its way to the visitors' center, and who snatched a velociraptor out of the air just as was leaping toward Alan, Ellie and the children.

The game warden, Robert Muldoon.
Had been sounding an ominous tune.
Led Ellie to shed.
But ended up dead.
His courage we could not impugn.

Dr. Grant gave the children protection.
From T Rex they hid from detection.
When they managed to enter
The visitors' center
Raptors moved in that direction.

The raptors were quick and were clever.
To escape them was quite an endeavor.
But a T Rex surprise
Caused the raptors' demise.
Their departure would be now or never.

The excitement did have a great cost.
As four different people were lost.
With the danger abated.
Hammond's mood was deflated.
For his plans, 'twas a sure holocaust.

Jurassic Park II – The Lost World

Four years after the mishap on Isla Nublar, Ingen (short for International Genetic Technologies, Inc.) was awash in red ink. John Hammond, sobered by the disaster at Jurassic Park, was still the head of InGen, but had become an environmentalist. He summoned Ian Malcolm and explained that while Isla Nublar had been the location for public attractions, the "factory floor" had been on Isla Sorna, eighty miles away. The dinosaurs were bred on Isla Sorna and later transferred. Hammond explained that the Isla Sorna facility had been decimated by a hurricane, had been abandoned, and that the animals had been released to fend for themselves. Hammond planned to send a 4-person team to the island to document the animals so that he could use the evidence to rally public support to isolate and preserve the island.

Four years later the plot it did thicken.
John Hammond had plans he would quicken.
Ingen's stock had sure tanked.
Hammond now was outranked.
Of his nephew's new plans he did sicken.

Though Ingen's fortunes did swerve.
Hammond showed a consummate nerve.
In spite of his severance.
He had a new reverence
He wanted the island preserved.

First he'd wanted to cause a sensation.
And to give the park goers elation.
But he made a big leap.
Now he wanted to keep.
All the dinosaurs safe from predation.

Hammond wanted a public appeal.
Had to show that the dinos were real.
To effectively plead.
Lots of pictures he'd need.
Then he felt he could rally some zeal.

Hammond's nephew, Peter Ludlow, convinced InGen's board to remove his uncle in favor of himself. Ludlow planned a very well-equipped mission to Isla Sorna. His plan was to capture several species of dinosaurs and to transport them to San Diego. There, in an amphitheater originally started by Hammond, InGen could set up a display that would presumably draw crowds and bail out the company. Ludlow hired African big game hunter Roland Tembo to spearhead the mission. Roland did not want money, but rather sought the right to hunt a male Tyrannosaur.

So Ludlow convinced Ingen's board.
From Hammond to sever the cord.
Dinosaurs that they'd capture.
Would give them great rapture.
When their company's stock price had soared.

To Isle Sorna Ludlow sent a mission.
They were greedy and had no contrition.
The animals fled.
And were captured or dead.
(Ludlow went there with big ammunition).

Roland Tembo acquired great fame.
In Africa hunting big game.
Hunters admired him
And so Ludlow hired him
To help Ingen fulfill its aim.

Said Roland, "I'll help with your mission."
But I harbor a greater ambition.
Risk I must confront.
So a T Rex I'll hunt.
It would bring my best dreams to fruition.

Hammond also sent a team to Isla Sorna. Ian Malcolm refused Hammond's request to join the team until Hammond informed him that his girlfriend, Paleontologist Sarah Harding, was already there. Malcolm accompanied field equipment expert Eddie Carr and video documentarian Nick Van Owen to Isla Sorna. It would later be revealed that in addition to photography, Nick was affiliated with *Earth First*, a radical environmental activist group. Hammond hired him to use sabotage if needed to thwart Ingen's plans to capture animals and remove them from the island.

Hammond also assembled a team.
They arrived just in time it did seem.
But while they were at work.
Ludlow's team went berserk.
What unfolded was like a bad dream.

Ian's crew sort of sat in the bleachers.
While Ingen's men captured some creatures.
The dinos they caught
Would then stateside be brought
To give their exhibit great features.

But Van Owen had come well-equipped.
And the locks on the cages he clipped.
Through the spaces that gaped
All the dinos escaped.
In the bud Ingen's plans had been nipped.

Roland used a device we'd detest.
Grabbed the infant T Rex from its nest.
They set it as bait
Then sat down to wait
To accomplish the goal he'd professed.

But the hunt was quite soon interrupted.
When chaos in camp had erupted.
Dr. Harding and Nick
Pulled one heck of a trick
When the infant T Rex they abducted.

Nick freed the infant T Rex that Roland used as bait, and convinced Sarah to bring the baby to their trailer to stabilize its broken leg. Ian protested, but the procedure was already done, and the infant's parents arrived. The adult T Rexes were not grateful that Sarah had treated and released their infant. They pushed the trailers over the cliff. Ian, Sarah and Nick managed to escape, but Eddie was killed by the Rexes while supporting his team. Both Hammond's team and Ludlow's team were disadvantaged and without communications equipment.

The young Rex's leg it was broken.
(To repair it was merely a token).
Ian surely did fret
As the bone they did set
He knew Rex's ire was awoken.

Ian's warnings were surely not heeded.
The adult Rexes came unimpeded.
Though their child was returned
Ian's fears were confirmed
To dismantle the camp Rex succeeded.

Bad luck to both teams had been handed.
And they all found themselves rather stranded.
They'd retreat from the beach
Attempting to reach
A facility that was abandoned.

During their forced march from the coast toward the facility in the Island's interior, Nick engaged Roland in conversation, trying to fathom Roland's motivations. Nick saw Roland's rifle unattended, and we later found out that Nick had removed the shells.

But by Rex their withdrawal was tracked.
Then finally they were attacked.
In all the confusion
caused by that intrusion
Roland found that his shells had been hacked.

Roland could not perform execution.
Which had been his intended solution.
Though he had been a skeptic
A strong neuroleptic
Became a right fine substitution.

T Rex was subdued and yet breathing.
And Roland was quietly seething.
Ludlow was upbeat.
An objective he'd meet
Higher stock prices he'd be retrieving.

Despite all the death and duress.
Ludlow deemed the sortie a success.
With T Rex on display
Many people would pay.
And the whole world Ingen would impress.

Ludlow felt that the adult T Rex and its infant would be a sufficient display to salvage Ingen's fortunes. But the Rex decimated the ship's crew on route to San Diego, then escaped from the ship to wreak havoc in the city. Ian and Sarah, having previously witnessed the adult T Rex's strong parental instincts, decided to use the infant Rex to lure the adult back to the ship. Ludlow was determined to at least keep the infant Rex in his possession. When Sarah and Nick deposited the infant Rex in the ship's cargo hold, Ludlow tried to retrieve it, leading to his demise.

They felt their detractors had caviled.
To San Diego they traveled.
Thought they were on a roll.
But they lacked good control.
And their plans then really unraveled.

When Rex ran amok in the city.
Events there were surely not pretty.
Ludlow was dismayed.
Plans were disarrayed.
Then Ian and Sarah got gritty.

The juvenile Rex they did steal.
To the instincts of Rex they'd appeal.
Led Rex on a chase.
Left the baby in place.
In the cargo hold Rex they would seal.

Ludlow had greed in his eyes.
Felt the infant T Rex was his prize.
He went down in the hold
(Not too smart but quite bold).
And it led to his grisly demise.

We're not sure what anyone learned.
But Ingen had really been burned.
With the episode done
Hammond's aim had been won.
To the island the Rexes returned.

J.K. Rowling and her Harry Potter Series

J.K. Rowling created a universe in which witches and wizards lived in a secret society. They lived alongside of, but were often hidden by spells from, from non-wizarding folks, who were termed "muggles." Talented young prospective witches and wizards were accepted to Hogwarts School of Witchcraft and Wizardly at age 11, to begin seven years of training.

A whole universe she created,
Making many young readers elated.
The stories she told
Were intriguing and bold.
And book prices soon were inflated.

She wrote about wizards and witches.
To heal cuts they used spells and not stitches.
Their school was a castle.
But not without hassle
As some of them had evil itches.

Harry Potter's parents were murdered by the evil Lord Voldemort when Harry was an infant. Voldemort tried to kill Harry as well but, due to his mother's love, Voldemort's curse rebounded and stripped him of his power. It would take him fifteen years to regain power. Harry was taken by Hogwarts' headmaster, Albus Dumbledore. to the home of his aunt and uncle, Vernon and Petunia Dursley. Dumbledore left a note, asking the Dursleys to raise Harry, and to inform him of his pedigree. The Dursleys, who doted on their son Dudley, treated Harry very badly and vowed to keep him from the magical world. When Harry was eleven, he was accepted to Hogwarts and, despite the Dursleys' resistance, he was rescued from their clutches by the school's gamekeeper, Rubeus Hagrid. Per Hagrid's instructions, Harry boarded the Hogwarts Express at King's Cross in London.

Harry Potter had grown up quite shielded.
Did not know of the powers he wielded.
When informed of his birth.
Did not take it with mirth.
Until to the truth he had yielded.

Great confidence he could not feign
When he first rode to school on the train.
This world was so new.
There was so much to do.
And so much new knowledge to gain.

Ronald Weasley was in the next seat.
(A very nice fellow to meet).
He would be a fast friend
From the start to the end.
They would be a tough combo to beat!

Another new friend was Hermione.
Her intellect hardly was tiny.
Though at first her exterior
Had an air much superior
She was clever and quick and not whiny.

Upon arrival at Hogwarts, a magical hat was placed on new students' heads. The sorting hat peered into their minds and assigned them to one of four houses. Harry's first year had begun.

Into houses at school they were sorted.
It determined with whom they consorted.
Incantations were spoken
There were rules (some were broken)
But from school they were rarely deported.

The wizarding world had been broken.
And Harry was more than a token.
Only he could defeat
The worst wizard you'll meet.
In a prophesy it had been spoken.

The main event of Harry's first year was his thwarting, with help from Hermione and Ron, Voldemort's attempted return to power. Voldemort had been assisted by Professor Quirrell, whose body he shared.

Hogwarts was the name of the school.
(Not a name to entice us to drool)
The dark arts defense teacher.
Had a very strange feature.
He was serving as Voldemort's tool.

The Sorcerer's Stone was protected.
But by Voldemort Quirrell was infected.
With great nerve and friends
Harry fought to the end.
And Voldemort's rise was deflected.

Harry's second year featured stopping another attempt by Voldemort to return. At the Dursleys, a creature Harry had never encountered – a house elf – discouraged Harry's return to Hogwarts. The elf, Dobby, said evil would transpire at school. Voldemort, named Tom Riddle when a student at Hogwarts fifty years earlier, tried to return through his own diary, which had been placed into Ron's sister's cauldron. Riddle wreaked havoc at school using a huge snake called a basilisk. In a hidden chamber far below the school, Harry killed the basilisk and, by impaling the diary with the snake's tooth, he dispatched Riddle.

When Harry went home for the summer
The Dursleys, of course, were a bummer.
Petunia's a shrew.
Vernon sure had no clue.
And, if possible, Dudley was dumber.

Harry was feeling dejected.
When an elf showed up quite unexpected.
He said evil and fear
Were expected that year.
He said Harry should leave school neglected.

A basilisk (snake of a kind)
Through the pipes of the school it would wind.
Fear and panic arose.
Would the school have to close?
It left petrified people behind.

The snake was by Riddle directed.
The mood of the school he infected.
He was oft filled with wrath.
But was glad when his path
And Harry's, by chance, intersected.

Riddle's presence emerged from a book.
A diary he'd left as a hook.
He was evil and bold.
Ginny's mind he controlled.
As he would anyone's who would look.

Lord Voldemort was the new name
Riddle fashioned to win himself fame.
But he thirsted to know
Fifty years ago
What had taken him out of the game.

Harry's parents Tom Riddle dispatched.
But by love he was then overmatched.
When he tried to kill Harry
His curse it did parry.
And his body and powers were scratched.

Harry fought and he killed Riddle's snake.
Then he tried Ginny Weasley to wake.
When the book he impaled.
Riddle's presence there failed.
As the spell he had managed to break.

Once again Voldemort was defeated.
And his power again was depleted.
But he still had the knack
In two years, he'd be back.
Too evil was he, and conceited.

On route to Hogwarts for Harry's third year, the train was boarded by dementors, the foul creatures who serve as guards at Azkaban prison. The dementors were searching the train for Azkaban escapee Sirius Black. Harry fainted in the presence of a dementor, which was then repelled by Professor Remus Lupin. Lupin dispatched the dementor via a Patronus charm.

Dementors cause victims to re-experience their worst memories, and Harry had experienced his parents' murder. Professor Lupin taught Harry how to perform a Patronus, which required a very happy memory.

We learned that Sirius Black was Harry's godfather, and had been unjustly held at Azkaban prison for betraying Harry's parents and killing many muggles. The real culprit was Peter Pettigrew, a former friend of Harry's father. Pettigrew was an Animagus (a wizard who could transform himself inro an animal – in this case a rat). Pettigrew had been living as Ron's family's pet rat for twelve years. Harry discovered the truth as the school year ended. Though Sirius was not legally exonerated, Harry and Hermione freed him.

A foul creature known as dementor
Can pull your emotions off center.
The technique they employ
Can remove all your joy.
To repel one you'll need a good mentor.

Remus Lupin was Harry's new teacher.
Under moonlight he'd roam as a creature.
He taught Harry a charm
To dementors disarm.
Joy would be an essential feature.

And alas, Voldemort was not through.
Help would come from one Pete Pettigrew.
He was homely and fat.
Was disguised as Ron's rat.
There was nothing bad he would not do.

Harry's godfather, Sirius Black.
Had really been stabbed in the back.
Pettigrew was a slime.
Framed Black for his crime.
After wreaking a vicious attack.

Much as Ron Weasley's rat he had learned.
Till he had his disguise overturned.
When he was discovered.
O'er him punishment hovered.
So to Voldemort he then returned.

Harry's fourth year at school was dominated by the tri-wizard tournament, in which he became an unwilling contestant. Three wizarding schools convened at Hogwarts for the tournament. Each school would be represented by one champion, selected by a magical vessel called the "Goblet of Fire." Harry wanted to be a face in the crowd and to watch the tournament, and did not submit his name. However, due to the machinations of an infiltrator working on Voldemort's behalf, after three names had been revealed, Harry's name emerged as a fourth contestant.

Voldemort's supporters were called "death eaters." A death eater named Barty Crouch, Jr had escaped from Azkaban, and imprisoned and impersonated professor Madeye Moody. He rigged the tri-wizard tournament so that Harry would be transported to a graveyard where Voldemort, assisted by Pettigrew, would use Harry's blood as a key ingredient in a spell that would bring him back to full power. Harry escaped, but the dark lord had returned.

Harry wanted to be a spectator.
Did not count on a foul infiltrator.
As to who was elite
And allowed to compete
The Goblet served as arbitrator.

Voldemort would dare start afresh.
With Pettigrew's aims his did mesh.
Though his powers weren't stale.
His body was frail.
He required a spell, blood and flesh.

Crouch Junior, another death eater.
Helped Voldemort just as did Peter.
Had Madeye in the brig
The tourney he'd rig
And the portkey became a two-seater.

With Cedric and Harry transported
A new body Voldemort sported.
From the evil landscape
Harry did then escape
So the goal to kill Harry was thwarted.

Harry's fifth year at school was a frustrating one for him. He and Dumbledore were not believed that Voldemort had returned. The Ministry of Magic installed Dolores Umbridge to teach defense against the dark arts at Hogwarts. She was also later named Hogwarts High Inquisitor. Umbridge was rigid and cruel, and taught no defensive skills. Harry's friends, impressed with his ability, persuaded him to teach them secretly in a place called the Room of Requirement. They called themselves "Dumbledore's Army." The lessons went well, and Harry even managed to teach the Patronus charm, advanced magic used to repel dementors, the foul creatures who serve as guards at Azkaban. When Umbridge discovered them, Dumbledore took responsibility for their secret work and left, rather dramatically.

Their confidence felt like a bonus.
But the mission was surely an onus.
It all seemed worthwhile
And Harry did smile
When Ginny performed a Patronus.

Harry's sixth year at school was eventful. Voldemort and his supporters were gaining power. Harry happened on a copy of a potions textbook that had handwritten marginal notes that helped him excel for the first time at that discipline. Significantly, Harry helped Dumbledore discover that Voldemort, via a series of murders, had sequestered seven parts of his soul in objects called "horcruxes." All the horcruxes would have to be destroyed if Voldemort were to be permanently defeated.

Harry had been having visions. It come to light that the visions were due to a connection between Harry's mind and Voldemort's. When Voldemort became aware of this, he was able to plant images in Harry's mind. By implanting an image that Harry's godfather had been captured, he manipulated Harry into traveling to the Hall of Mysteries, where Harry and his friends had to battle the death eaters. The scene culminated in a standoff battle between Dumbledore and Voldemort, and in Minister Cornelius Fudge arriving in time to finally see that Voldemort had indeed returned.

Harry accompanied Dumbledore on a dangerous mission to retrieve one of Voldemort's horcruxes. When they returned, Severus Snape dispatched Dumbledore with the killing curse. It would be a year before Harry would learn that Dumbledore had been dying from a curse encountered while handling another horcrux, and that Snape had killed him on Dumbledore's own orders.

Harry liked being in motion.
To this subject had not shown devotion.
But the marginal notes
In the book that he totes
Helped him make an exceptional potion.

Voldemort his own soul he did split.
And he hid it away bit by bit.
If each piece were discovered
And its essence smothered
His return would no longer be lit.

It turns out there was a connection.
(Not characterized by affection).
Voldemort's mind
Was with Harry's aligned.
It was used for a cruel misdirection.

When Dumbledore's death we perceived.
At Snape we were sorely aggrieved.
It turns out that the deed
Was by Albus decreed.
Though Harry was more than just peeved.

Harry, Ron and Hermione did not remain at school for their seventh year. Instead, they went on a quest to find and destroy Voldemort's remaining horcruxes.

Voldemort had taken over the Ministry of Magic, and inquisitions were conducted to persecute witches and wizards whose parents were not both of wizarding descent. Voldemort eventually assembled an army to invade Hogwarts, intending to kill those who would not defect to his side. In a final showdown, Voldemort hurled a killing curse at Harry. The curse deflected off Harry's disarming charm, and Voldemort perished. His horcruxes had all been destroyed and his demise was thus permanent.

When Pettigrew helped him to power.
His influence really did flower.
There were cruel inquisitions
With evil decisions.
Under his rule good wizards did cower.

Good and evil would have a collision.
In essence, there'd be a decision.
Would suspicion and fear
Be the history we'd hear?
Or would justice create a revision?

Prophesy told the intention.
That these two remain in contention.
Four times they'd do battle
Voldemort, he did prattle.
But Harry accomplished ascension.

When the last confrontation ensued.
Voldemort was defiant and rude.
When their spells had been cast
It was Voldemort's last.
Bringing in a victorious mood.

The Universe, the Earth and Life

I am working on a book entitled A Brief History of the Universe, the Earth and Life – Illustrated with Limericks. I thought it might be interesting to include a few of those limericks in this volume. Each of the limericks will require some substantial introductory material.

The Universe Begins

The Universe begins about 13.8 billion years ago (That is 13,800,000,000 years ago). The event that starts the Universe is typically referred to as "The Big Bang." That term was initially used in derision by an astronomer who opposed the theory.

We live on the surface of the Earth in a nearly constant gravitational field and we travel at very modest speeds. Our intuitive view of the way the world works has developed in that environment. And Sir Isaac Newton's classical physics is consistent with our intuitive sense of the world. However, Albert Einstein's special and general theories of relativity, as well as quantum mechanics, have revealed a Universe that defies the "common sense logic" that derives from our day-to-day experience.

What astrophysicists tell us is not easy to understand from the point of view of our experience. That is, the Universe did not expand into empty space that surrounded it. Rather, space-time itself began to expand.

Intuition has been countermanded.
Though in no way are we reprimanded.
There was no empty space
Into which things could race.
It was spacetime itself that expanded.

Edwin Hubble and the Expanding Universe

The prevailing belief 100 years ago was that the whole universe consisted of one vast sea of stars. Observers had noticed spiral patches of light among the stars. They termed them "spiral nebulae" and did not imagine that they were separate galaxies.

During the 1920s, Edwin Hubble built on the work of Henrietta Leavitt and studied "Cepheid variable stars," which vary in brightness. Leavitt had found a direct relationship between the periods and luminosity of these stars. With the stars true luminosity estimated, the ratio of luminosity to apparent brightness gives an estimate of distance. Hubble studied Cepheids in the Andromeda nebula and found that Andromeda is extremely distant and is a separate galaxy.

When light passes through a prism, it is separated by wavelength and we see a rainbow. This is the heart of the spectroscope, an invaluable tool of astronomers. The rainbow of colors is an emission spectrum, and dark lines through the rainbow is an absorption spectrum, which gives evidence of atoms between the source and our instruments.

Hubble examined the spectra of several galaxies. He was confused by the absorption lines, as they did not look familiar. In what must be termed a stroke of genius he realized that the absorption lines were shifted toward the red end of the spectrum. The frequency of the light waves coming from other galaxies had been stretched out. This is the same phenomenon that you have noticed when a vehicle with a siren approaches you and then moves away. As it approaches, the pitch of its siren goes up, and as it recedes the pitch drops down. Hubble reasoned that the light waves were stretched out because other galaxies are moving away from us at a very high speed. In 1929, Hubble published his observation that the farthest galaxies are moving away faster than the closest ones. This insight became known as Hubble's Law. Since galaxies are moving away from each other, astronomers concluded that our universe is expanding, transforming our understanding of the Universe.

It causes us not any trouble
That the Cosmos expands like a bubble.
It's a thrill just to know.
And a debt we do owe
To astronomers like Edwin Hubble.

Nuclear Fusion in the Sun's Core

Life on Earth depends on energy from the Sun. Energy is produced in the Sun's core when protons fuse together, releasing energetic gamma rays. As you are aware, opposite charges attract and like charges repel one another. Due to the electromagnetic force, protons therefore repel one another. However, there is a force greater than electromagnetism. That is the "strong nuclear force," which binds atomic nuclei together. Though very strong, the strong force acts over extremely short distances. The density in the Sun's core is extreme, and protons are squeezed together with such pressure that the strong force takes over and they fuse. Two protons together form a helium nucleus. When they do so, gamma radiation is released.

It is certainly not an illusion.
And I don't mean to cause you confusion.
Under pressure and heat.
Protons stick when they meet.
In a process called nuclear fusion.

The Fate of Our Sun

The Sun is making helium out of hydrogen. In four to six billion years, the Sun will run out of hydrogen in its core. The core will collapse until high pressures will fuse helium nuclei together to make carbon nuclei. But our Sun is not massive enough to fuse anything heavier than carbon.

When the Sun fuses helium into carbon, it will swell, become a red giant, and its outer layers will reach Earth's orbit. After millions of years, helium fusion will stop. With no outward flow of radiation, the Sun's atmosphere will collapse until it reaches the size of the Earth. It will be hot at its surface but there will be no nuclear fusion. It will be a hot, glowing ball of carbon - essentially a glowing cinder. That is the end stage for stars the mass of our Sun. It is called the white dwarf stage, and the Sun will remain in that stage for many billions of years, perhaps until the end of the Universe as we know it.

A star with the mass of the Sun.
Will make carbon and then will be done.
Heavy stuff it won't make.
Not for anyone's sake!
More massive stars will have that fun.

Massive Stars Disperse Heavy Elements via Supernovas

The Universe has stars of widely different masses. Supermassive stars can have hundreds of times more mass than our Sun. Supermassive stars have immense pressures in their cores and fuse elements faster than do stars like our Sun. And, they do not stop after fusing helium into carbon. They go through a series of oscillations, in which they fuse heavier and heavier elements. When they fuse iron, however, the situation becomes dicey. The fusion of iron absorbs heat, rather than producing it, and the core of the star collapses violently and rebounds in an intense explosion called a "supernova." During such a supernova event, all the elements, all the way through uranium, are created.

Super massive stars will not stop.
Up the ladder of atoms they hop.
But when iron they fuse.
Supernova ensues.
It is quite a bit more than a pop!

Supernova explosions create heavy elements and scatter them throughout interstellar space. This enriches the interstellar medium with heavy elements, which make later generations of stars and planets. If stars did not fuse heavy elements, the Universe would be uninteresting. Can you imagine a Universe with no elements other than hydrogen and helium? Without heavy elements, there would be no complex compounds. Without complex compounds, there would be no life.

So, you see, elements are created.
By stars that have masses inflated.
Without all the matter
To the cosmos they scatter.
Our Universe would be ill-fated.

Interstellar Gas and Dust Condense

Interstellar clouds of gas and dust are initially not dense enough to form stars and planets. Something must cause them to "bunch up" and to develop regions dense enough for star formation. Imagine a room full of cigarette smoke. Imagine a fan turned on at one side of the room. The fan creates a "shock wave," as it were, of moving air. When the shock wave hits the nearest smoke, it pushes that smoke into the smoke behind. By the time the shock wave of air reaches the far side of the room, the smoke has become quite a bit denser.

A similar process may take place in interstellar gas/dust clouds. The shock wave is not provided by a fan, however, but by a stream of particles coming from a supernova. When the gas and dust become very dense in a region, its mutual gravitation becomes stronger, and it eventually collapses so densely that the temperature and pressure at its center are great enough for nuclear fusion to begin. A new star is born.

Gas and dust in regions immense.
Need a process by which to condense.
A wave from a blast.
Can bunch them up fast.
From contraction there is no defense.

The Early Solar System

During its early history, the Solar System was very chaotic. Although most of the mass was concentrated in the center, there was considerable debris left in orbit about the young Sun. Starting with small dust grains, matter began to stick together in small bits, which grew larger with time. The process by which particles in orbit about a center of mass gather and grow is called "accretion." Bodies in orbit about the young Sun and in the process of becoming planets are called "planetesimals."

When in orbit around the new star.
Whether dust or the size of a car.
When these fragments meet.
They collide. They accrete.
Planetesimals: that's what they are.

Planetesimals join, and they grow.
Through collisions, they get hot and glow.
That's how Earth got her start.
Bit by bit, part by part.
Till she grew to the size that we know.

The Formation of the Moon

The advent of computer modeling has allowed scientists to run simulations of the evolution of the Earth/Moon system. It is now believed that, during the early era of the Earth's formation, the Earth experienced a collision with an object the size of Mars. A large amount of material was blasted into orbit about the Earth. Over millions of years that material coalesced into the Moon. The Moon has a very small nickel/iron core, which is consistent with this model.

The Moon posed one heck of a riddle.
With models math experts did fiddle.
One scenario fit.
We must have been hit!
By an object that hardly was little.

That a body into the Earth tore.
Is supported by evidence more.
When Moon reached completion.
By the process accretion.
Little iron was there at its core.

The Early Bombardment

During the early era of the formation of the Solar System, there were many bodies in orbit, and their orbits were chaotic. Once the inner, rocky planets – Mercury, Venus, Earth and Mars – as well as Earth's Moon, had attained considerable mass, their gravitational attraction caused them to be bombarded by many smaller bodies.

In Earth's orbit and in its surrounding.
Rocky bodies and comets abounding.
In the Sun's inner region.
These objects were legion.
And the Moon and the Earth took a pounding.

The Late, Heavy Bombardment

Planetary scientists estimate the ages of craters on the Moon, Mars and Mercury. Based on their analyses, cratering appears to have slowed down for a few hundred million years, and then accelerated again in what has become known as "the late, heavy bombardment."

All celestial bodies have a gravitational effect on one another, with various effects. For instance, have you ever wondered why the Moon's rotation period exactly matches its orbital period? That is, it takes the Moon 28 days to revolve around the Earth, and it takes the same 28 days for it to rotate once on its axis. Therefore, the same side of the Moon always faces us. This process is known as gravitational locking.

The planets Jupiter and Saturn appear to have had gravitational effects on one another as they orbited the Sun. Whenever they were close together in their respective orbits, they would "tug on each other." Ultimately, their mutual tugging caused them to be close to one another every time Saturn completed one orbit around the Sun and Jupiter completed two. Their orbits are said to have become "resonant." Some researchers believe that the total gravitational effect of the Jupiter/Saturn combination disturbed the orbits of many bodies in orbit around the Sun. Some bodies may have been ejected into longer orbits, while others may have been flung in toward the inner Solar System. It is possible that the resonance of the orbits of Jupiter and Saturn was the cause of the late heavy bombardment.

It seems cratering was inflated.
When two giant planets related.
They tugged on each other
Like sister and brother
And their orbits became resonated.

Origin of Earth's Oceans

We look out at Earth's oceans and we see them as immense. However, the oceans account for only about one four-thousandth of the mass of the Earth. Keeping that in mind is important as we consider the theories of the origin of Earth's oceans. Comets are often described as "dirty snowballs" or "snowy dirtballs," and they contain a great deal of water. That is why they develop a tail when approaching the Sun; some water is vaporized by the Sun's radiation. The prevailing theory has been that comets delivered the water that created Earth's oceans and lakes.

Comets are dust grains and ice.
For us, that's incredibly nice!
Earth would not have quivered.
As ice was delivered.
For our seas the amount would suffice.

The Origin of Life

Somewhere between 4.0 billion and 3.4 billion years ago, life made its first appearance on Earth. We do not know precisely how life got its start. At some point, complex molecules became encased in cell membranes. Our knowledge of life's development prior to that point is very murky. After that threshold was reached, our knowledge becomes clearer.

A billion years after its birth.
Life started somewhere on the Earth.
Just how is not certain.
Deep time is a curtain.
Of evidence there is a dearth.

For the past few decades there has a major increase in the amount of research time and dollars devoted to the origins of life. The earliest research indicated that the simplest organic molecules can easily be assembled if elements and compounds such as methane and carbon dioxide are mixed with water and subjected to an electric current equivalent to lightning. In addition, in a letter to a colleague, Charles Darwin had once speculated about life's origins having perhaps been "somewhere, in a warm little pond . . ."

These two ideas led to the belief that life had begun in a "primordial soup" of organic molecules in the ocean. Although there are still proponents of that idea, many other possibilities for life's origins have been advanced. Your author is impressed with evidence that life began undersea, in hot spots known as hydrothermal vents.

Some say life began in the ocean.
Where organic soup made a potion.
Other theories abound.
Did life start underground?
These debates spark tremendous emotion.

Research into the origins of life is sometimes divided into "bottom-up research" and "top-down research." Bottom-up research involves laboratory work. In elaborate experiments, using expensive materials and equipment, basic elements and compounds are subjected to the high pressures and heat that may have been present on the primordial Earth. The goal is to create organic molecules complex enough to be convincing that they are on a path of increasing complexity that could eventually lead to living cells.

The "bottom-up" method is neat.
We use pressure, organics and heat.
To try to assemble
Some things that resemble.
The stuff of cells, mammals and wheat.

Many origins of life researchers argue that simple organic molecules needed some type of structure, or scaffolding, to help them to assemble into the longer chains of molecules needed for life. For instance, the idea has been advanced that clay soils, which are arranged in a specific layered structure, could have provided such a scaffolding.

Could minerals have been so used?
As longer organics were fused?
Could the answer be clay?
(We don't know to this day).
Warring theorists are not amused.

The Great Oxygenation Event

Earth's early atmosphere probably had no oxygen in it, compared with the twenty-one percent oxygen atmosphere we enjoy today. The first life forms capable of photosynthesis probably evolved somewhere around three billion years ago. The process of photosynthesis produces oxygen, and abundant stromatolites and cyanobacteria created atmospheric oxygen. As oxygen increased, it combined with iron to form iron oxide, or "rust." When oxygen production peaked and declined it left alternating layers of red and grey deposits. Evidence of the great oxygenation event can be found in these so-called banded iron formations across the Earth.

Complex life needed an invitation.
More than just a mere incantation.
At life's first cafeteria
Cyanobacteria
Caused the great oxygenation.

Snowball Earth

As strange as this may seem, there is now significant evidence that Earth has experienced eras in which polar ice caps reached the tropics, creating "snowball Earth." How could such a thing happen? And, once it did happen, what could have ended deep freeze?

First, billions of years ago, the Sun was only seventy percent as luminous as it is today. Earth remained warm due to the insulating effect of the methane in its atmosphere. Early life forms, called archaea, produced methane, which as a greenhouse gas is twenty times as effective as carbon dioxide, the greenhouse gas that we talk about today. The methane-rich atmosphere kept Earth habitable when the young Sun was less luminous.

Life forms developed photosynthesis and Earth's atmospheric oxygen rose. Oxygen stripped carbon from methane (CH_4), forming carbon dioxide (CO_2). CO_2 is only one twentieth as effective a greenhouse gas as methane. Glaciers reflected the Sun's energy back into space, the Earth cooled, and glaciers advanced and radiated more energy into space. This is a positive feedback loop. Glaciers advanced to the equator. The entire Earth was frozen over, but life, probably single cell life only, was not extinguished.

Earth's climate has had some wild swings.
Due to feedback loops of certain things.
We've had ice, pole to pole.
These events take their toll.
Thankfully, to existence life clings.

Some scientists have argued that the snowball Earth scenario could not have happened, as there would have been no way to turn things around. However, volcanism would have been the key. The Earth was, and still is, releasing heat left over from its formation 4.6 billion years ago. Volcanoes release immense amounts of carbon dioxide, and this would have led to an increase in the greenhouse effect. A new positive feedback loop would have ensued, with glacial retreat, warmer Earth, more glacial retreat, et cetera.

You may wonder what melted the ice.
Volcanoes in this case were nice.
C-O-2 in the air.
Caused a greenhouse, and there
Lay the answer that sure did suffice.

The Principle of Superposition

Early investigators into the evolution of the Earth and its biosphere relied a great deal on the positions of various types of rock, and the fossils accompanying them, in the layers of the Earth. Nicolas Steno was a 17th century Danish man who studied natural science and formulated principles of stratigraphy. The principles seem obvious to us through the lens of current day knowledge, but it was ground-breaking (pun intended) at his time.

The principle of superposition states that layers of sediment above are younger than sediments below. The principle of original horizontality states that even when we find strata that are vertical or diagonal, they were originally deposited in a horizontal plane. The principle of cross-cutting relationships states that when we have layers of sediment with a different type of rock thrusting through it, the invading rock is newer than the sediment through which it is thrust. Biologists and Earth scientists have had to corelate many different types of evidence to arrive at a description of the history of Earth and its life forms.

The principles of stratigraphy have been immensely important to the history of science.

Before I renew the rendition.
Of the tale of life's early condition.
To know we have thirst.
What came last? What came first?
The concept of superposition.

The Cambrian Explosion

The era from 542 million years ago to 251 years ago is known as the Paleozoic Era, and is divided into six periods. The period from 542 million to 488 million years ago is referred to as the Cambrian Period. The fossil evidence appears to reveal such a great increase in the diversity of life that it has often been referred to as "The Cambrian Explosion." The distinguishing feature of Cambrian life forms is the appearance of hard parts, such as shells and bones, by a process called bio-mineralization.

Our early knowledge of the Cambrian Period comes primarily from a huge discovery in British Columbia called the Burgess Shale, discovered by fossil hunter

Charles Walcott. Walcott made his first discovery there in 1909, returned there year after year, and by 1917 had collected 65,000 specimens.

Although Walcott quarry is now high above sea level, evidence indicates it was an undersea environment in the Cambrian. A vast array of life forms has been fossilized there. During the Cambrian Period, life essentially "experimented with a wide variety of body plans," many of which later disappeared. However, most of the phyla we see on Earth today had their origins during the Cambrian, so its importance cannot be overemphasized.

A locale called the Burgess Shale.
Tells a truly remarkable tale.
Life branched out with great change.
Body plans, new and strange.
Life had really begun to set sail.

If we could travel back to the Cambrian, we would find the land devoid of any sign of life. We would not see a blade of grass or a patch of moss. The land was essentially sterile. It would not be until the Silurian

Period that life would finally establish a foothold on land.

But the lands were as bleak as could be.
All the life forms were still in the sea.
When would life crawl on land,
to touch rocks, to touch sand?
For a long time it was not to be.

The Ordovician Period

The Ordovician period lasted from 488 million to 444 million years ago. The Ordovician has been described as "a tropical paradise." Life flourished only in the seas. No life form had yet made it out onto the land. The Ordovician saw the first modern-type coral reefs, which were every bit as extensive as today's reefs.

Life forms in the Ordovician period were interacting more with their environment than had the Cambrian forms. They were burrowing deeper into the ocean sediments. Some anchored themselves to the sediment, and some would detach themselves and float freely in the water, perhaps seeking food.

Though described as a tropical paradise, the Ordovician was not destined to last. The first of the five major life extinctions that the Earth has endured occurred at the end of this period. Although it is not a certainty, climate change has been identified as the likely culprit that caused this extinction.

After Cambrian came Ordovician.
Warm and tropical was the condition.
Who'd first leave the sea?
Which life form would that be?
Which phylum would make the transition?

The Silurian Period

The Silurian Period was the third of the six periods of the Paleozoic Era. It lasted from 444 to 416 million years ago. Worldwide temperatures were rising again, and shallow oceans covered many landmasses. Once again, the numbers of lifeforms proliferated, with the first appearance of bony and jawed fish.

The climate was generally warm and stable in the Silurian Period, in contrast to the glaciers of the late Ordovician before and the extreme heat of the Devonian that would follow. This led to the colonization of land by the first plants. Of the photosynthetic organisms, lichens were probably the first to cling to land. Erosion, along with the decay of lichens, led to the buildup of the first true soil. The first plants to have an upright stalk would have been a few centimeters high. The first known air-breathing animals were arthropods. Millipedes, centipedes and the earliest arachnids first appear in the Silurian. Thus, arthropods, and not vertebrates, were the first animals to venture forth onto land.

Is it ego, or is it Darwinian
To see vertebrates having dominion?
Saying, "Backbones in place,
Made our kind win the race."
Is in fact a misguided opinion.

The Devonian Period

The Devonian Period occurred from 416 million to 360 million years ago. It is often known as the "Age of Fishes," though there was also significant evolution of plants, insects and other animals.

By the mid-Devonian, there were two new groups of fish that had bones, teeth and gills. The Ray-finned fish were the ancestors of most modern fish. The Lobe-finned fish were more common during the Devonian but largely died out. Though they became nearly extinct themselves, the lobe-finned fish were of particular importance. All birds, mammals, reptiles and amphibians were a diversification of early tetrapods, which in turn probably evolved from Lobe-finned fishes able to use their muscular fins to feed in the new wetland environments. The earliest known tetrapod is Tiktaalik, considered to be the link between the lobe-finned fishes and early amphibians. Tiktaalik was probably mostly aquatic, "walking" on the bottom of shallow water estuaries. Its hind limbs were stronger than those in front, suggesting it was able to propel itself out of the water

The exhibits in our Smithsonian.
Not to mention our physics Newtonian.
Would never have been.
Were it not for the fin
Of the beasts from the middle Devonian.

The Carboniferous Period

The Carboniferous Period lasted from 360 to 299 million years ago. The name "Carboniferous" reflects the most famous attribute of the Carboniferous period: the massive vegetation that cooked today's vast reserves of carbon, in the form of coal and natural gas, over a few hundred million years.

Carboniferous coal was produced by trees that grew in vast lowland swamp forests. The growth of these forests removed massive amounts of carbon dioxide from the atmosphere, leading to a surplus of oxygen. Atmospheric oxygen peaked around 35 percent, compared with 21 percent today. This may explain the giant arthropods that emerged. The size reached by insects and similar creatures is limited by the amount of air they can breathe. In the oxygen-rich, swampy Carboniferous forests, there were dragonflies with two-and-a-half-foot wingspans, canary-size flies, and the number of insect families increased from 1 or 2 to more than 100.

Over millions of years, the organic deposits of plant debris from this era formed extensive coal deposits. Humans still burn this coal today.

The giant swamp forests splendiferous.
Led to growth of huge insects pestiferous.
When we dig and we dole
All our gas and our coal.
Know it came from the time Carboniferous.

The Permian Period

The Permian period was the last of the six periods of the Paleozoic Era, and it ended in a vast extinction. The Permian lasted from 299 to 251 million years ago. All the Earth's continents bunched up, and the emerging supercontinent of Pangaea presented severe extremes of climate, as the central regions were far from the ocean and dry.

On land, the giant swamp forests of the Carboniferous were dried out. Mossy plants that depended on spores for reproduction were replaced by the first seed-bearing plants. Early reptiles flourished, and other mammal-like reptiles known as therapsids eventually became warm-blooded. These more metabolically active reptiles became the dominant land animals of the late Permian, and led to dinosaurs, birds and mammals.

The Permian period ended suddenly 251 million years ago. The Permian extinction - the most severe extinction event in the planet's history - wiped out more than 90 percent of all marine species and 70 percent of land animals. Various theories seek to explain this mass extinction. Some scientists think a series of volcanic eruptions pumped so much debris into the atmosphere that the sun was blocked out, causing a temperature drop, preventing photosynthesis, and thus causing food chains to collapse. Nonetheless, life on Earth is resilient, and surviving species diversified into the life forms of the next era – the Mesozoic.

The Permian's vast habitation
Met an end of uncertain causation.
That era's distinction
(its sudden extinction)
Led to diversification.

The Triassic Period

The Triassic Period followed the great mass extinction at the end of the Permian, and was the first period of the Mesozoic Era. The Triassic's span is considered to be 251 million to 199 million years ago. Until this time, the most plentiful life was in the oceans, but the Triassic saw a period of rapid diversification on land.

The first mammals evolved near the end of the Triassic Period. Early mammals of this era were small, shrew-like creatures a few inches in length. They may have been primarily nocturnal, and probably ate plants and insects. Most were egg layers, but they had fur and nursed their young.

The Triassic Period ended with in the fourth of the Earth's five major extinction events. Approximately thirty percent of Earth's species became extinct, and the causes are not fully understood. Among the suspects are gradual climate change, sea-level fluctuations, and ocean acidification.

Was it ocean acidification
That brought about life's degradation?
Did changing sea level
Those life forms bedevil?
We're not certain about the causation.

The Jurassic Period

The Jurassic Period (199 million to 145 million years ago) was characterized by a warm, wet climate in which lush vegetation and abundant animal life flourished. Many new dinosaurs emerged, and in great numbers. During the Jurassic, the breakup of the supercontinent Pangaea began and accelerated. Laurasia is the name given to the northern half, and Gondwana to the southern half.

Today, the name "Jurassic" awakens images of the successful book and movie, *Jurassic Park*. Dinosaurs were dominant on land during the Jurassic Period.

However, many dinosaurs featured in *Jurassic Park*, such as Triceratops and Tyrannosaurus Rex, did not evolve until the Cretaceous Period, long after the Jurassic. The largest land animals of all time, gigantic sauropods, lived during the Jurassic. They included iconic dinosaurs such as Diplodocus, Brachiosaurus and Apatosaurus. The plated stegosaurs, another icon of dinosaur lore, were also a Jurassic herbivore. Allosaurus was probably the largest predator of the period. The Jurassic also saw the origination of the first birds, including the well-known Archaeopteryx. The sea was teaming with life as well. Many readers will recall seeing pictures of plesiosaurs, who had broad bodies, long necks and four flipper shaped limbs, and ichthyosaurs, which were a more fish-shaped reptile.

The Earth, to be sure, was revolving.
The dinosaur world was evolving.
Sauropods were a classic.
Roamed in the Jurassic.
Pangea was slowly dissolving.

The Cretaceous Period

The Cretaceous was the third and last period of the Mesozoic Era. It lasted about 79 million years, from the end of the Jurassic Period to the Cretaceous-Paleogene (K-Pg) extinction event of 65.5 million years ago. In the early Cretaceous, the continents were in very different positions from today, but by the end of the period, the continents were moving closer to their modern configuration.

The Cretaceous was another banner period for dinosaurs. Large herds of plant-eating dinosaurs thrived during the Cretaceous. These included duck-billed dinosaurs such as Iguanodon, heavily armored turtle-like Ankylosaurs and ceratopsians, including the iconic Triceratops. Theropods, including Tyrannosaurus Rex, were the top predators. Though emblematic of the age of dinosaurs, Tyrannosaurus rex appeared only during the last few million years of the Cretaceous.

The Cretaceous period and the Mesozoic era came to a screeching halt 65.5 million years ago. It was known for decades that a mass extinction had taken place, but a probable cause only became evident a few decades ago. A heavy concentration of the heavy element iridium was found by Walter and Luis Alvarez in a clay layer between the Cretaceous and Paleogene strata. Iridium is rare on Earth but common in meteors and asteroids. Glen Penfield, a geophysicist working for a Mexican oil company, discovered evidence of a vast underground crater near Chicxulub, a town on Mexico's Yucatan Peninsula. These were the "smoking guns" that proved that Earth had in fact been struck sixty-five million years ago. The results would have been catastrophic, and may have included worldwide fires and huge dust clouds cutting off photosynthesis and snuffing out life.

They didn't just lie down and quit.
In the fossil remains, it is writ.
The iridium layer
Shows they had not a prayer.
When a giant space boulder did hit.

It was just ten kilometers wide
Hit the Yucatan right in its side.
Devastation it brought.
And we have been taught
That 7 of 10 species died.

The Paleogene

The Cenozoic era follows the mass extinction that ended the Mesozoic era. The first period of the Cenozoic is the Paleogene (65.5 to 24 million years ago), during which dinosaurs, pterosaurs, and giant marine reptiles were conspicuously absent. Mammals no longer had to occupy niches safe from predatory dinosaurs. Rodent-size mammals emerged and, over the next 42 million years, they grew in number, diversity and size. As the period came to a close, life-forms still common today filled the seas, dominated the land, and had taken to the air.

During the Paleogene, oceans widened as the continents continued to drift farther apart, heading toward their modern positions. Europe and North America parted, and Australia finally broke away from Antarctica. The climate significantly cooled and dried, and oceans dropped from their cretaceous levels, draining most interior seas. Sharks emerged as the top ocean predator, and squid and other soft-bodied cephalopods became numerous. Perhaps the biggest development in the seas was the appearance of whales in the mid-to-late Paleogene.

The dinosaur world terminated.
The great inland seas had abated.
The world now had whales
Ocean mammals with tails.
On land mammals proliferated.

The Neogene

The Neogene Period is the second of three divisions of the Cenozoic Era. The Neogene Period is the time period from 23 million to 2.6 million years ago. The continents continued their inexorable movement, drifting apart in some areas but crashing together in others. India continued to merge with Asia at great speed (3 inches per year), causing the rise of the Himalayas that continues today. Similar forces caused the formation of the Alps and Pyrenees in Europe and the Rocky, Sierra Nevada, and Cascade Mountains in North America. New, higher terrain altered air circulation and weather patterns, and the climate grew drier and cooler. Snow fell on the high mountains, locking up water as snow and ice. The Arctic ice cap grew thicker. Dropping ocean levels exposed land bridges.

In the highlands was much falling snow.
It was pressed into ice as we know.
With water contained.
The sea levels drained.
Between continents bridges would grow.

Connections between continental land masses enabled animals that had evolved in isolation to migrate. Ocean life changed, and kelp forests grew in cool waters. Animals such as otters evolved to live in the environment the kelp provided. Megalodon, the largest of all sharks at nearly fifty feet in length, appeared 16 million years ago.

The ocean levels were dropping.
Earth's crust would move on without stopping.
There were mounts on the rise.
A shark grew to great size.
Across continents species were hopping.

Forests gave way to grasslands in the cooler and drier weather. But hardy grasses contained less nutrition, so grazing animals evolved stronger teeth. To survive in the open, grazers became faster and roamed in herds, so predators had to adapt as well.

Dry grasses were harder to chew.
Harder teeth then the plant eaters grew.
The advantage conferred
When they stayed with a herd
Was that predators' stress did accrue.

But the predators retaliated.
Their senses and speed were inflated.
Species evolve.
With new problems to solve.
Their old ways would soon be outdated.

The Pleistocene
(First epoch of the Quaternary Period)

The Quaternary Period is the third period of the Cenozoic Era, and has traditionally been divided into two epochs: the Pleistocene (1.8 million years ago to 11 thousand years ago) and the Holocene (11 thousand years ago to today). However, there is a growing body of thought that we are in a third epoch of the Quaternary: the Anthropocene, which is seen as the epoch in which human activity has been the dominant factor in the development of Earth systems. The Quaternary Period is noted for its intervals of glaciation and interglacial warming periods, as well as the emergence of humankind.

Temperatures were cooler everywhere on Earth during the Pleistocene. But the climate did not stay the same throughout the entire epoch. The Earth warmed and cooled and polar ice caps advanced as vast glaciers, and then retreated. Scientists have identified over 60 cycles of glaciation during the Pleistocene. The entire Quaternary Period, including the present, is referred to as an ice age due to the presence of at least one permanent ice sheet (Antarctica).

Polar ice advances and retreats may not be random. For instance, over the last million years, the tilt of the Earth from its orbital plane has varied between 22.1 and 24.5 degrees. The time between maxima is about 41,000 years. This is one of three cyclical patterns that together are called Milankovitch cycles.

The Earth did get cool then it heated.
The glaciers advanced and retreated.
Did the tilt of Earth
Give these changes their birth?
Sixty times the cycle repeated.

The Holocene

The last major glacial advance was about 18,000 years ago, and the glaciers retreated about 11,000 to 10,500 years ago, ushering in the Holocene epoch. Some scientists say that we are still in an ice age and the current warming trend is just an interglacial period or temporary retreat of the polar ice.

As Earth entered a warming trend, glaciers retreated and tundra gave way to forest. As the climate changed, the very large mammals that had adapted to extreme cold, such as mammoth and wooly rhinoceros, became extinct. Humans had been dependent on these "mega mammals" for food. We therefore had to switch to smaller game, and to increase our gathering of plant-based food to supplement our diet.

Evidence indicates that about 11,000 to 10,500 years ago, human beings began inventing the processes that would change the planet forever: purposeful agriculture. Life changed drastically when our ancestors began to grow grains. First, once harvested, grains could be stored, and were therefore a repository of wealth. This led to many changes in the way people related to one another. Eventually, it led to taxation. Another change was that instead of living in small, migrating foraging groups, people could live more permanently in towns. One result of this was increased disease.

We used to hunt food using stealth.
From which may have flowed better health.
What we used to seek growing
We found ourselves sewing.
And it led to a storehouse of wealth.

The Anthropocene

Anatomically modern human beings have existed for just 300,000 years. This represents less than one ten-thousandth thousandth (1/10,000) of the history of life on our planet. Yet our impact on the planet is so great that scientists around the world are recommending that our period in Earth's history be named the "Anthropocene" – the age of humans.

It appears species are becoming extinct 100 times faster than they would have without human impact. Populations of large wild animals have more than halved since 1970, while the human population has doubled. Five major extinctions have been identified in the history of life. The reign of the dinosaurs ended at the fifth major extinction, the close of the Cretaceous Period sixty-five million years ago. Many scientists call what is happening now the "sixth mass extinction."

Human beings have caused alteration.
Of the planet's diversification.
Is a mark of distinction
To cause an extinction?
Or should we seek modification?

Attention Deficit Disorder

The following five limericks describe the subjective experience of having attention deficit issues:

To do well in school was my goal.
And at times I could get on a roll.
But then I would slip
And my grades they would dip.
'cause my mind I just could not control.

In class the discussions I'd follow.
My analysis may appear hollow.
When I was alone.
I wanted to moan.
'cause in random thoughts my mind would wallow.

On good habits I'd set my intention.
(Though always with some apprehension).
I'd sit down to study.
My mind would get muddy.
I could not sustain my attention.

How others could do it I wondered.
The voice in my mind often thundered:
"If your mind is that hazy.
It's just that you're lazy!"
It must be my fault that I blundered.

I forget things and then my heart's sinking.
My self-esteem's currently shrinking.
I left on the heat.
My phone's under the seat.
I'm a spaceshot is what I keep thinking.

The following eleven limericks have to do with remedies – skills and awareness persons may use to be better organized and to feel better about themselves:

Then I met a psychologist, Mike.
Who said "I know just what you're like.
I will show you some tools.
If you follow the rules.
In a better direction you'll strike."

Obligations will line up in queue
And this method will help you get through.
I'm quite sure you may
Have a much better day.
Just remember to "stop-scan-and-do"!

It's attention, it's not plague bubonic.
And there's no need for music symphonic.
If you mislay your key.
Why not listen to me.
Develop a helpful mnemonic.

For cell phone we'll use letter "C"
"K" will help you remember your key.
For your wallet and air.
A and W, there!
So "WACK" your mnemonic will be.

When I have some place I must go.
I often arrive and think "Whoa!"
I left with such speed.
I left things that I need.
There must be a plan I don't know.

Think "RCA Victor" Mike said.
You will not have to have so much dread.
It's a simple device.
It will often suffice.
You'll feel great about using your head.

R, relax, there's no need to be stewing.
C, complete what it is you were doing.
A, attend to the thing
You most need to bring.
V, velocity – Go! Time's a brewing.

Almost everyone has places in their homes - drawers, closets, boxes - that are so packed with stuff that they dread opening them. Everything in them has become useless. Imagine a kitchen drawer that has many useful items. But there are so many, packed in so tightly, that you have trouble seeing what you want. Even if you see it, you cannot extract it without some other item getting dragged out with it and clattering to the floor. Here is the limerick:

You may feel it's a pain and a bore.
With too many things in a drawer.
When an item you pick.
Something to it may stick.
When you lift them they fall on the floor.

You probably know at least one or two persons who have difficulty keeping their house, apartment, or desk neat and uncluttered. You may even know someone who expresses frustration due to his or her inability to stay on top of things. The biggest reason for procrastination is that the task feels too big, complicated or formidable at the moment we are facing it. The "Do Ten Things" method is a good method for just about everyone and not just for persons with ADHD. We can take what would otherwise be a formidable task and cut it down to a non-formidable, approachable size.

One very common example is straightening up a house or apartment. When it looks too formidable to attack, proceed like this. Put your athletic shoes back in the closet and say "one." Put yesterday's newspaper into the recycling bin and say "two." Take a jacket off the arm of the sofa and hang it up and say "three." Take a coffee mug out of the living room, put it in the kitchen sink and say "four." When you get to ten, stop! If you practice "Do Ten Things" often, you will never face a huge task, and things will stay neat and organized.

My drive to do tasks gets deflated.
When the task appears too complicated.
If I just do ten things
Satisfaction it brings
And fear of tasks is dissipated.

Persons who feel disorganized sometimes try so hard to become perfectly organized that they become frustrated and give up. And, people who are disorganized often say mean things to themselves. In almost all endeavors, striving for perfection is impossible. It is also unnecessary and wastes our energy.

For example, if everything that goes in your refrigerator goes in helter-skelter, you will lose items and will be frustrated trying to find what you need. But ff you have a special place for six of ten things that go in your refrigerator, you will not have a problem finding the other four in the rest of the fridge. Moreover, if all the papers and documents on your desk are in one big pile, you will waste time and get frustrated finding a paper you need. But if six of ten papers are in labelled file folders, you will easily find something else in the small pile that is left. You will say better things to yourself. I call this the "sixty-forty principle."

It always ends up with dejection
Whenever I strive for perfection.
Getting sixty percent
Is much better time spent.
For myself I can feel some affection.

Imagine that you are in the cereal aisle of a supermarket, searching for your favorite brand of toasted oats. There is a sea of cereal boxes in front of you, in three rows, stretching far to your left and right. You hope to find your brand quickly, so you play your luck. You look at the top shelf to your right.

No luck there. You quickly look down to your left. Same result. You continue to let your eyes dart back and forth until you finally find your brand. By this time, you may be feeling tense and disorganized. If you have panic attacks, you may be starting to have symptoms.

The alternative is the gentle eye sweep method. Begin by looking at the top shelf on your far left. Sweep your eyes from left to right, at a moderate pace, keeping your eyes on the top shelf. When you reach the far right, if you have not found your favorite toasted oats, drop your eyes to the middle shelf and sweep from right to left at a moderate pace. Once again, if you have not found your oats, drop your eyes to the bottom shelf and sweep your eyes back to the right. You may find your target early in the process, or late in the process. Over the course of shopping for many items, on average you will spend the same amount of time as you would have by playing your luck with the eye dart method. However, your brain will be quieter. You will feel calmer and more relaxed, and you will feel clever. And, you will have trained yourself to think and behave in a more effective way.

If my eyes keep shifting their angle.

My nerves will soon be a jangle.

If I use the eye sweep

My composure I'll keep

My emotions won't get in a tangle.

Classic Star Trek

There have been at least five Star Trek series. The original series is often called "Classic Start Trek." It is also sometimes known as "TOS" - for "the original series." It was cancelled after three years, but would later gain wide popularity and became a cultural icon.

In real life, we cannot exceed the speed of light. Albert Einstein informed us that as velocity gets closer to light speed, mass increases until no more acceleration is possible. Countless subsequent experiments in physics, many with particle accelerators, have confirmed Einstein's assertion. The nearest star to our Sun, Proxima Centauri, is 4.3 light years away. Thus, if we could travel at one tenth the speed of light (a speed still beyond our capability), it would take us forty-three years to reach it. A plethora of great science fiction has been written with topics consistent with this limitation. But to appeal to popular culture, the originators of Star Trek conjured up "warp drive" to allow wide ranging travel.

We cannot go faster than light.
And that makes our range rather tight.
More stories would thrive
If they conjured warp drive.
And they did so to viewers' delight.

The special effects could be spotty.
And the doctor would sometimes seem dotty.
But who doesn't know?
When you'd much rather go.
You can just say, "Please beam me up, Scotty!"

Enterprise was the name of the ship.
Her Captain Jim Kirk was quite hip.
They had a translator
Their comm-u-ni-cator
Opened right up with a flip.

The ship's science officer Spock
Thought emotions were really a crock.
He was rarely a bore.
He used logic galore.
With a mind meld your thoughts he'd unlock.

The Enterprise captain was Kirk.
His duties he never would shirk.
His role was quite serious.
He could be imperious.
As Captain, I guess that's his perk.

The ship's doctor had the name "Bones."
He often would deal with unknowns.
To assess your disorder
He'd use a tricorder.
When intense he'd use whispering tones.

Uhura, at home at her station.
Would relay to the home federation.
The news of their flight
Whether triumph or plight
By subspace com-mu-ni-cation.

The series was more than a token.
To think freely our minds may have woken.
But was it not strange
In all their wide range
That by aliens English was spoken?

Star Trek: The Next Generation

The original Star Trek series was cancelled after three seasons. At that time, it was considered a failure, but later was immensely popular in reruns. The series became a cultural icon and spawned a series of very successful movies. Years later, another series, **Star Trek: The Next Generation**, was aired, with a whole new cast of characters.

The Captain was Jean Luc Picard.
In ways he was quite avant-garde.
Though somewhat austere
Never showed any fear
By his crew was held in high regard.

Will Riker was next in command.
His resume he'd not expand.
He disdained a promotion.
To Picard had devotion.
Had tough situations in hand.

She ship had a counselor: Troi.
(You would not mistake her for a boy!)
Of Betazoid line
She could sense your design
Her talents Picard would employ.

An android held rank of commander.
His role could not have been much grander.
Precise in his actions
Could not use contractions.
He always would speak with great candor.

Mr. Data was played by Brent Spiner.
His role on the ship was not minor.
He was somewhat forlorn
That he had not been born
But was built by a brilliant designer.

Worf's role on the spaceship was tactical.
The lieutenant was really quite practical.
At times enigmatic.
He was charismatic.
Had fighting skills that were fantastical.

Worf had been Klingon by birth.
Was serious and rarely showed mirth.
Though by humans adopted.
Would not be co-opted.
Of courage he had not a dearth.

Chief engineer Jeordi La Forge.
Did not let blindness stop him, by George!
His visor detected
All wavelengths reflected.
And a fine career path he would forge.

Star Trek: Deep Space Nine

Still another series in the Star Trek Universe is **Deep Space Nine**. The setting is a space station in orbit near the planet Bajor. The Bajorans had previously been conquered by a race called the Cardassions (not to be confused with the Kardashians), who built the space station as a mining processing facility and called it Terok Nor. When the Federation took over the station, they renamed it Deep Space Nine.

Nearby Bajor we have Deep Space Nine.
First built as adjunct to a mine.
With their captors' abort
Federation support
Was for Bajor a lot more benign.

Nearby the station and Bejor was a stable wormhole that allowed travel between two quadrants of the Galaxy. The Bejorans worshipped extradimensional beings called *The Prophets*, who inhabited the wormhole. The idea of a wormhole is a convenient one for creators of science fiction. However, our understanding of physics does not allow it. First, though mathematically possible, a wormhole would be submicroscopic – on the order of 10^{-33} centimeters – not even wide enough for a hydrogen atom. Secondly, the immense gravity required to form a wormhole would also create a time dilation, and travel through the wormhole would take more time and not less. Nonetheless, just as with the devices of warp drive and subspace, devising navigable wormholes gives creators of science fiction more realities to explore.

A wormhole is quite a device.
The idea does writers entice.
Though by physics prohibited
To those uninhibited
It adds to a story some spice.

Captain Sisko, in charge of the station.
At the end of a foe's occupation.
His duties he'd bear
And be honest and fair.
And rejoice in Bajor's liberation.

Having long fought for Bajor's resistance.
Nerys Kira was filled with persistence.
Loved Bajor's tradition.
Accepted the mission:
Gave Benjamin Sisko assistance.

O'Brien, a fine engineer.
Knew his trade; it was soon very clear.
In charge of all ops.
He could not afford flops.
In his job on the stellar frontier.

Chief Odo, a clever shape-shifter.
Will catch you if you're a shop lifter.
At this scheme you may scoff.
From a quadrant far off.
From his origin he'd been a drifter.

Star Trek: Voyager

The Federation starship Voyager, commanded by Captain Kathryn Janeway, pursued a ship that was part of a rebel group called the Maquis. Both Voyager and the Maquis ship were hurled into a different quadrant of the Galaxy by a powerful alien technology called the Caretaker's array. Voyager and the Maquis ship were stranded 70,000 light years from home, which is about seventy percent of the diameter of the main disc of the Milky Way Galaxy. Captain Janeway convinced the Maquis to join her Federation crew and to work together to attempt the long voyage home.

The Maquis crew had to disband.
And serve under Janeway's command.
With problems she'd wrestle
Commanding the vessel.
It was not at all what she had planned.

Chakotay the Maquis had led.
Now served under Janeway instead.
He kept his esteem.
They made a good team
As back toward their quadrant they sped.

At security Tuvok did serve.
As a Vulcan, he did with tough nerve.
Though clearly devoted.
At one point demoted.
So the chain of command he'd observe.

For promotions Janeway was sincere.
She made Torres chief engineer.
Half Klingon by birth
She would soon show her worth.
As she served she became less austere.

Seven of Nine was quite blessed.
When she was from Borg service pressed.
Through many a wrangle
The camera angle
Would seem to show her at her best.

Harry Kim was a young ensign slated
For ops surely not antiquated.
He had a design
On Seven of Nine
An attraction that would be frustrated.

Tom Paris served at flight control.
His performance his mates would extoll.
In space he'd not tarry
Torres he would marry.
As Voyager sped toward its goal.

The Doc, holographic creation.
Would appear and would seek information.
If you speak your words faster
When there's a disaster
Your life will not face expiration.

As the series progressed Doc was changing.
As his programming was re-arranging.
At times a technique
Gave him striking mystique.
As some distances he was seen ranging.

Limericks with Friends, Family & Others

I know someone who goes by the nickname "Honus." We see each other frequently, and we also talk and text. Honus complimented my knack for quickly composing limericks, and I texted:

I don't know if rhymes are a bonus.
Is it clever, or is it an onus?
Of rhymes I keep thinking
Without even blinking.
I've a knack, or at least, so says Honus!

I have many patients who are very emotionally reactive to things going on around them. They often feel frantic in response to life's demands. I have told these individuals that they may feel like a cork on the surface of the ocean, being pushed around by wind and waves. I suggest they imagine themselves sinking down below the wind and waves, where they can still see their tasks and obligations on the surface, but can address them without the feeling of being buffeted about. I have provided this limerick:

If the surface has frothed and has bubbled.
And the chaos appears to have doubled.
I want you to think
And remember to sink
Where the water is still and untroubled.

One of my invited brunch guests described a screen door that had warped. He said he would get to it, but not until after attending my brunch. So, I texted:

A Lexington fellow named Steven.
Said, "My screen door is warped; it's not even!"
I will fix it someday.
But not right away.
'cause on Sunday for brunch I'll be leavin'"

.

Someone had work stress due to changing shifts and assignments. His doctor put him on leave, and he sought new employment. Other issues emerged. He was watching three-to-four hours of sports on television every day, causing relationship stress, weight gain and lack of attention to professional development. I texted him as follows:

His last job he found quite oppressive.
The schedule shifts were excessive.
I am happy to state
On his next he'll do great!
(If his sports-viewing is not obsessive!).

I know someone who is very concerned about his son Josh (pseudonym). Josh has obsessions about cleanliness and about environmental toxins. He told his father he had been running away from buses to avoid breathing the fumes from their exhaust. In addition, though Josh appeared to be seeking employment, he did not appear willing to accept a job. I wrote:

Of toxins and dirt he sure fusses.
But working would sure have its pluses.
If from work he'll demure
Of one thing we'll be sure.
It won't help that he's running from buses.

I know a person whose son has been having severe emotional problems to the point of being suicidal. His son was hospitalized for ten days, and while in the hospital he was encouraged to write a list of fifty reasons to live. I commented that these reasons would lose their impact if he were to read all fifty at once. I suggested it would be more effective to read three at a time, and to think carefully about the three. I texted my patient the following:

The reasons to live number fifty.
And happiness sure would be nifty!
Try if you please,
To review them in threes.
It would be more effective and thrifty.

He replied with a text: "I knew there was a reason I liked you."

I was talking with a fellow who tends to overthink everything, and to question himself incessantly about his choices and his performance. In addition, he tries to do things perfectly which, of course, results in frustration as we can do nothing perfectly. I described to him an analogy of rowing a boat. I told him if he sat in the boat trying to adjust the oars so the blades would be exactly, perfectly vertical, he would never start rowing. However, if he gripped the oars so they appeared to be vertical and started rowing, he would be making progress. While describing this to him I wrote the following limerick and handed it to him.

Of his life he is being reflective.
Perhaps he is too introspective.
The idea I am sewing
With image of rowing
Could help him to be more effective.

Later the same session he brought up the concept of "flow," which is the subject of the book *The Psychology of Flow* by Mihaly Csikszentmihalyi. (Yes, that is the author's name. It is pronounced "Mike Cheek-sent-me-high"). I suggested to this guy that his obsessive thinking would interfere with achieving flow. I wrote the following limerick and handed it to him.

The wine of life he'd be drinking.
At times his hopes seem to be sinking.
For a great sense of flow
Is a place we can't go
If we're too bottled up in our thinking.

Someone recently spent hours frantically searching for a lost wallet. We can easily understand his dismay, as a lost wallet means that credit cards must be cancelled and driver's and other licenses must be replaced. The wallet turned up, and in the weeks that followed he often commented how satisfying it was to have his wallet safely tucked in his pocket. Therefore, from his point of view, I wrote the following:

My light bulb may dim in its socket.
My bike chain may fall off its sprocket.
But whatever goes wrong
I am fine just as long
As my wallet is safe in my pocket!

Fantasia and T Rex

In 1940 Walt Disney Productions released a movie entitled "Fantasia." It was an animated movie of artists' impressions of the works of classical music composers. Though primitive by today's standards, the animation was avant-garde at the time and was considered quite marvelous.

One of the vignettes depicting Igor Stravinsky's "Rites of Spring" is a scene involving a battle between a tyrannosaur and stegosaur. According to the knowledge of the day, such a confrontation may have been plausible. However, we now know that Stegosaurus went extinct by the end of the Jurassic Period 145 million years ago, and Tyrannosaurus Rex evolved during the last few million years of the Cretaceous Period, approximately 67 million years ago. Tyrannosaurs really lived *closer in time to us* than they did to stegosaurs!

"Fantasia" was truly audacious.

But the dinosaur scene was fallacious.

Stegosaurus, though classic,

Lived in the Jurassic.

While T Rex lived in the Cretaceous.

What is a Scientific Theory?

The word "theory" has a meaning in common parlance, and a completely different scientific meaning. In common speech, a "theory" can mean a speculative idea with no evidence. In common speech you may say, "I have a theory that we do not exist, but that we are thoughts in the mind of a gigantic interstellar octopus." We could never test such an idea. Wild ideas and fanciful speculations can be fun, but they are not theories in the scientific sense.

In science, we start with a hypothesis. - an explanation of events with some evidence and is a starting point for further investigation. A hypothesis must be subjected to investigation – either observation of natural events or controlled experiments. If the evidence does not support the hypothesis, then the hypothesis is dropped, or new experiments or observations are planned.

When observations or experiments consistently support a hypothesis, a tentative theory is born. Even then, results are published and other researchers try similar experiments or make similar observations. When many observations or experiments support the tentative theory, a full-fledged scientific theory is in place.

I'll admit that I become weary
When people misuse the word "theory."
If truth is your quest
Put ideas to a test!
Of untested stuff please be leery!

Can't You Drive Better than That?

Maybe I am just a skeptic, but by my observations, people's ability to anticipate, to be efficient, and to be patient are sorely lacking when they are behind the wheel.

The highway is really a sight!
Drivers always seem ready to fight.
Their behavior's obsessive.
They're much too aggressive.
They tailgate and pass on the right.

With traffic laws people will tinker.
And sometimes it's really a stinker!
When you're changing your lane
Do not be insane!
Is it so hard to turn on your blinker?

Poem about the Camel

The following is not a limerick, but rather just a whimsical seven-couplet poem. A friend of mine was on a tour in Morocco, and she emailed me that she would be riding a camel. I asked her if it were a Bactrian Camel or a Dromedary, and she replied that she did not know. I then emailed her the following:

I really think you should be wary
while hanging 'round a dromedary.

Please do attend! Keep sharp your wits!
Because, you see, at times he spits!

Behind his head, before his rump
The dromedary has one hump.

If you see two humps on a camel,
It may be a Bactrian Camel.

The fable is it has a pump
To store its water in its hump.

When really, it's in all its cells
That all the extra water dwells.

Will this info bring you happier times?
Who knows? But I like making rhymes.

About the Author

Michael Slavit is a psychologist in private practice. He received his Bachelor's degree in Psychology at Brown University, his Master's degree in Counseling at the University of Rhode Island and his Doctorate in Counseling Psychology at the University of Texas at Austin. He is board certified in Behavioral and Cognitive Psychology by the American Board of Professional Psychology, but he considers his most important credential to be the confidence of his patients.

Dr. Slavit has a variety of writing interests. He is the author of:

Embracing fitness
Train Your Wandering Mind: Coping with ADHD
Lessons from Desiderata
Your Life: An Owner's Guide
Cure Your Money Ills: Improve Your Self-esteem
    through Personal Budgeting
Journeys of Imagination: Science Fiction short Stories
U.S. History Through a Prism

He has works in process, including

A Brief History of the Universe, the Earth and Life (illustrated with limericks)
My Life as a T Rex

Dr. Slavit treats patients for a variety of issues including depression, anxiety, ADHD, unresolved grief and health/fitness/weight. He believes that not all personal problems have to be viewed as emotional disorders, but may be more appropriately seen as inevitable problems adjusting effectively and happily to a complex and demanding world. Dr. Slavit has produced over a hundred handouts and brochures to help educate his patients.

References

Astronomy Magazine. Waukesha, WI: Kalmbach Media, many issues 1972 through 2022.

Blassingame, Wyatt. *The Look-it-up Book of Presidents.* New York: Random House, 2012.

Crichton, Michael, *Jurassic Park.* New York: Alfred Knopf, 1990.

Crichton, Michael. *The Lost World.* New York: Alfred Knopf, 1995.

Davis, Todd and Frey, Marc. *The New Big Book of U.S. Presidents,* Philadelphia: Perseus Books, 2013.

DeGregorio, William A. *The Complete Book of Presidents.* Fort Lee, New Jersey: Barricade Books, 2005.

Freidel, Frank, *Our Country's Presidents.* Washington, DC: National Geographic Society, 1981.

Hamilton, Neil A. *Presidents: A Biographical Dictionary*. 3rd Edition. New York: Facts on File, Inc., 2010.

Internet Resources
www.history.com
www.nasa.com
www.science.howstuffworks.com
www.space.com
www.wikipedia.org

Jenkins, Phillip. *A History of the United States.* New York: St. Martin's Press, 1997.

Nevins, Allan and Commager, Henry. *A Short History of the United States.* New York: Knopf, 1966.

Rowling, J.K. *Harry Potter ad the Sorcerer's Stone.* New York: Scholastic, 1997.

Rowling, J.K. *Harry Potter and the Chamber of Secrets.* New York: Scholastic, 1999.

Rowling, J.K. *Harry Potter and the Prisoner of Azkaban.* New York: Scholastic, 1999.

Rowling, J.K. *Harry Potter and the Goblet of Fire.* New York: Scholastic, 2000.

Rowling, J.K. *Harry Potter and the Order of the Phoenix.* New York: Scholastic, 2003.

Rowling, J.K. Harry Potter and the Half-Blood Prince. New York: Arthur Levine Books, 2005.

Rowling, J.K. *Harry Potter and the Deathly Hallows.* New York: Arthur Levine Books, 2007.

Slavit, Michael. *Train Your Wandering Mind.* North Charlston, South Carolina: CreateSpace Independent Publishing Platform, 2015.

Yenne, Bill. *The Complete Book of US Presidents.* Minneapolis: Zenith Press, 2016.

Made in United States
North Haven, CT
05 April 2023

35084215R00095